CARLO CARRETTO

# AND GOD SAW
# THAT IT WAS GOOD

translated by Alan Neame

ORBIS BOOKS

**Maryknoll, New York 10545**

The Catholic Foreign Mission Society of America (Maryknoll) recruits and trains people for overseas missionary service. Through Orbis Books, Maryknoll aims to foster the international dialogue that is essential to mission. The books published, however, reflect the opinions of their authors and are not meant to represent the official position of the society.

Originally published as *E Dio vide che era cosa buona* © 1988 by Editrice A. V. E., Roma (Italy)
English translation © 1989 by St. Paul Publications, Middlebreen, Slough SL3 6BT, England
U.S. edition published in 1990 by Orbis Books, Maryknoll, NY 10545

Typeset in England
Printed and manufactured in the United States

ORBIS/ISBN 0-88344-654-5

# Contents

# Introduction

## *Hymn to hospitality*

To be travelling one very hot day through an arid, sun-parched countryside and, as you go, to come across an oaktree with underneath it Abraham's tent and hear the words, *"My Lord, I beg you not to pass by without stopping"* (Gen 18:3), and then to be entertained in lordly fashion by the great patriarch, would give anyone pleasure.

To reach Zarephath (I Kings 17:10) in a time of drought and dearth and run into a poor widow, who for love of God bakes you a little cake with the last of her flour and the little oil remaining, and then puts you up in her house to save your life, as happened to Elijah (I Kings 17), is really good.

To crisscross half a world proclaiming the gospel, as St Paul did, and then arrive dead tired in Philippi to hear Lydia, a dealer in purple fabric of Thyatira, say, "If you have judged me to be faithful to the Lord, come and stay in my house" (Acts 16:14), is — no doubt about it — very good indeed.


Hail, divine hospitality!

Hail, human heart ever open to the needs of those we encounter on our way.

Hail, obedience to the word of Jesus; he said, *"If anyone forces you to go one mile, go two miles with him"* (Mt 5:41).

Hail, inexhaustible courage of the love that overcomes our individual absorption in self and invites us to hold the door open to the needs of our fellow-beings!

Hail, kindness of those who understand how to listen in silence!

Hail, heroism of those who welcome the life of a child coming to birth!

Hail, sublime fruitfulness of friendship!


Each of us has something apposite to say about this.

Nowadays people are judged rather by their capacity for loving and for giving hospitality to the poor than by being beyond reproach in discharging the duties of religion.

Like Abraham, like Elijah, like Paul, I too have something to say about hospitality.

Thanks to the merciful goodness of our God, I have devoted practically my entire life to proclaiming the gospel.

On every continent where I have been privileged to go and meet my brothers and sisters in the faith, I have seen amazing things.

And I keep seeing more.

And especially I see a new thing, filling me with joy: the Christian home becoming more and more *the Church in miniature*.

When I used to go to church as a boy, religious practice was essentially centred on ''the priest''.

The laity I knew, patronisingly described as *vulgus indoctus*, were still immature and inert, a flock of sheep, with a cleric on whose shoulders fell the full weight of the apostolate.

Then came a new age.

Beginning in the pontificate of Pius XI and increasingly through the reigns of Pius XII, Paul VI and John XXIII, a process of development took place on a vast scale within the Church.

The laity became aware of forming the Church and grasped the fact that their faith didn't merely urge them to acts of piety but required them to live out the gospel message in the world.

Everything became the material of religion: home, politics, social relations, job, life, love.

The Second Vatican Council — the most extraordinary religious event to have taken place in all the centuries of Christianity — effected the Church's transit from childhood to maturity, obliging everyone to see the Church as the *people of God* and no longer as a clerical pyramid.

This achievement was of enormous significance and in fact formed the theological basis for the new concept of church-and-world. Even though we haven't yet achieved in entirety what the new perspectives, afforded by the Council, may reveal, we have made a great deal of progress.

Without the presence of the laity and without a just, fruitful, balanced, loving collaboration between hierarchy and laity, the life, the activity of a Christian community, whether large or small, would be inconceivable today.

This is maturity!

This is the conscious response to the wealth of prophetic content in God's word, "*You are a people of priests*" (I Pet 2:9).

Yes, a people of priests, not people bossed by a priest.

The priestly task — that of living the life of Jesus in his absolute self-giving to the Father and of offering all earthly reality to the Father — is now the responsibility of all the baptised, in the unity of the Holy Spirit.

What may we not expect to see in the Church,

once this becomes a complete, mature, genuine fact?

There certainly won't be any more crises over lack of vocations, since from now on all vocations will be priestly!

No longer shall we have a Church expressing itself exclusively in terms of "rite" and "public worship", but a Church acting and making itself felt as the leaven in the dough, as the salt of the earth.


My readers will forgive me for having wanted once again to break a lance on behalf of my favourite topic: the presence of the laity in the Church.

It's because once again, now as my death draws near, I've had the joy of experiencing the beauty of brotherly love, of the genuine apostolate, that came to me through the vision of *the family as the Church in miniature.*

I had fallen ill . . . seriously enough to feel the total weakness of someone overpowered by pain and by days full of bitterness and poverty.

In this condition I was gathered up by a Christian family who carried me off to their house in the mountains, to see — which was more than kind of them — whether there was any chance of getting me better.

For two months I was treated with prodigious hospitality by Christians not only determined to make me strong again but eager to pray together and live together in an atmosphere of love and spiritual joy.

There, while thinking about myself and what had happened to me, the idea came to me that I ought to encourage all those people who feel alone or without support in their lives to break out of their loneliness and try and live the Project 'Church', meaning community, charity, prayer, through friendship and sharing.

"Woe to him who is alone," says the Scripture (Eccles 5:10), and how true this is!

And how true it is that we ought, while there is yet time, to commit ourselves with all our strength to holding the front-door open to the spreading of the gospel, to praying in common and to the wonders of forming the Church.

Then we shall find we aren't alone any more and friends will be like sons begotten in our youth, *"sharp arrows in the quiver"* who will help us, as Psalm 127 says, *"when the enemy comes to parley at the gate"*.


To those friends of mine in whose house I wrote it during my convalescence, I dedicate this book.

And as I dedicate it to them, so I dedicate it to all the countless couples and families I have known during my stint on earth, who have made me the gift at my passing of a dream fulfilled: *the home as the Church in miniature.*

CARLO CARRETTO

11

# PART ONE

# WHAT GOD HAS TO SAY
# ABOUT CREATION

# And God saw that it was good

When God created heaven and earth, he confidently pronounced that *"it was good"* (Gen 1:1).

And as though this were not enough, and perhaps thinking we might eventually come to doubt the truth of what he had said, he repeated the sentence seven times for good measure.

Speaking of the earth putting forth its shoots and plants, he said it was good; he said the same about the firmament of heaven giving light to earth; he said it too of the living creatures darting through the air and swarming in the waters, and encouraged them to be fruitful and fill the immensity of the seas and the canopy of the skies.

He said it too of the domestic animals, reptiles and beasts of the wild.

To conclude the litany, when speaking of the human race created in his own image and likeness, he added unhesitatingly that this was *very good*, and there he stopped since further he could not go and better he could not say.

To assert that heaven and earth are good, earthquakes notwithstanding, may be fair enough, but to say as much when speaking of human beings, with the additional *it was very good* into the bargain, must inevitably give us pause for thought.

Human beings aren't only Adam, they're Cain too; not only good but also perverse; they are the Mafia, the Camorra, lust, violence, darkness, war and things of this sort.

How are we to say of Judas, of the Nazis, of thieves, of rapists, of Nero, of me a sinner, that these are good?

Even if we stop at the earlier stages of the litany where it speaks of the natural world, we can hardly say with absolute conviction that everything in the garden is lovely.

The cloudburst suffocating me in mud and washing away the home I've built for myself with so much effort, the cancer confining me to a bed of pain year after year, the terrible effects of hunger on children in many, many parts of the world: these are things that make me wonder.

The garden of Eden where God placed Adam *"to till it and look after it"* (Gen 2:15) isn't always a bed of roses.

Tilling involves hard work . . . and how!

Looking after the garden isn't straightforward.

If only all the trees were fruitful!

But what are these wild ones for?

These poisonous ones, these twisted, useless ones?

All these elements of chaos I perceive in a work defined as good?

How is one to take a right view in matters so complicated and mysterious?

How am I to pick my way through such a mass of contradictions?

Nature isn't only the pretty, well-manicured lawn of some wealthy man's country-house, to be admired and enjoyed by people no longer aware of what it feels like to labour for a living; it's a hostile force all too often unleashing its train of parasites, beasts of prey, locusts, floods, droughts, epidemics, famine, cold, infant mortality, hail, frost and un-parallelled catastrophies.

And I'm supposed to tend and till all that?

How am I to prune the right branches, how free the good grain from the tares that stifle it?

How am I to set about taming all those wild

animals, all these microbes custom-built to vex and complicate my existence?

Nonetheless that's how things are, and God said *"this was good"* (Gen 1).


Did he do so to provoke us?

Did he do so to confound us?

The important thing is he did so, and I can't ignore what he may say.

I'm obliged to think about it: not for a few minutes either.

It will take my entire lifetime, and even that won't be long enough for solving the mystery.

I've recently been reading two books about Asia.

One of them was about what happened in China when the Cultural Revolution broke out under Mao; the other was about the horrors that took place in Kampuchea under the Pol Pot regime.

When young people, indoctrinated with Marxist ideology, are impelled by their very political innocence to try and create a new world free of evil, there are no limits to the barbarities they will commit.

The facts as set down defy one's powers of belief.

Millions of men slaughtered, women disembowelled, children trained to betray their parents and lie for the sake of the revolution, unburied corpses in monstrous killing-grounds: and this in a land which had evolved the highest, purest, richest tradition of devotion to the ancestral dead.

And all to make a new world, a clean, anti-bourgeois world, a world free of evil and injustice.

No one reading the story of the little Kampuchean girl Peuw, who is presented by Natalia Ginzburg as a reincarnation of the victim of Nazi violence Anne Frank, could refrain from shedding what tears compassion can still muster in sorrowing over the wickedness of human nature and in weighing its shame as against its supposed redemption.

The most impressive thing about these stories is that they are born of the intensity of one of the greatest attempts ever made to change the world and change it for the better.

We do well to remind ourselves that the often heroic atmosphere of the Russian Revolution was the product of eastern mysticism, rich in justice and love for the poor.

No one who reads *The Twenty-fifth Hour* by Georgiu can fail to be astounded at the dedication of the revolutionary, prepared to endure year upon year of prison and persecution in the hope of changing things in a country martyred by hunger and unjust rulers.

And this same revolutionary, purged from the cadres of the Party as a grain of sand might be from the gears of some machine, to be executed by a revolver-shot in the back of the neck in one of the many cells of the Lubyanka, will himself wonder in horror how human affairs can possibly degenerate to such a point as regards the leadership, having begun with so much good will, such love of justice.

Pol Pot, who in Kampuchea embodied the most lucid attempt to create a completely new society, didn't hesitate to assign the task of realising it to the young — the only people unsullied by the errors of the past and free of bourgeois culture and selfishness. And it was these same young people without a past, who were to commit crimes of the utmost brutality in the name of truth and the revolutionary creed.

It doesn't seem possible that reality could so quickly be stood on its head as it was in China

18

by the Cultural Revolution and in Kampuchea by Pol Pot.

And this is when, with infinite apprehension, we ask ourselves, "Human being, who are you?"

Has goodness no part in you?

Then how can your Creator say of you: *It was very good*?


This is indeed the problem and I must neither close my eyes to evil, nor undervalue God's word.

What was God intending to convey to me by the words *it was very good* with reference to the human being that he had created?

This is the great mystery of human nature, something I can't pass over in silence.

No, I can't evade it.

For it involves God's very credibility and my credibility which compels me to believe what he says.

I'm optimistic by nature, I like being optimistic and I like spreading optimism around me.

I'm disposed to credit God with being optimistic too, since I find it so easy to be so myself!

Hidden deep within me is all the strength of faith, and hope against all hope.

As well as this, there is love.

I love my God as I love no one else, and with love much progress is made even before setting out.

But I hope he too will have something to say to me in this debate.

I think that's important, particularly now when many values have collapsed, when many certainties have been eroded and when human beings are so frightened of one another.

We have reached such a breakdown in behaviour, we witness such infamous actions on every continent, even those least corrupted ones like Africa and South America, that they leave us breathless.

Immorality, abuse of sex, drugs, greed, injustice, abuse of power, thirst for riches, indifference to the common good, have reached such dimensions that we must question whether the human race can keep going much longer.

We are bemused by so much evil, and feel that the atom-bomb, that symbol of apocalyptic destruction lurking so terrifyingly on the human horizon, may in fact have already exploded deep within the human heart.

Can humanity manage to survive?

How long can this dehumanised, cruel, supposedly civilised behaviour go on?


Studying the word of God, I am struck by the sentence occurring in the Book of Genesis, which I have used as the title of this book: "And God saw that it was good" (Gen 1).

It fills me with optimism, with great confidence in human nature.

I want to ask its Author something very relevant to this.

I want him, through his Holy Spirit, to tell me what his real reason is for affirming that human nature is good and for showing his confidence in us, as his words bear witness, by unhesitatingly adopting us as his children and linking our eternal destiny to his plan of peace and happiness.

Can I ask this?

I can try.

I shall try and talk to him in simple terms, as a child talks to his father.

I shall do my best to avoid any of those cultural

or theological complexities devised to make conversation difficult.

Above all I shall keep firmly before me the eternal consideration dictated by humility that the truth about God is veiled in the sweet and ineffable grandeur of his mysterious being.

# Human beings, pay attention to me

You ask me what I meant when I said, "God saw that it was good".

I meant what I said, nothing more, nothing less.

I meant to say that creation was good and that, even if on one occasion I did feel sorry I'd made it, there's always been a Noah standing before me "*to find favour in my eyes*" (Gen 6:8).

And that's no small thing!

Furthermore, can you imagine a "non-creation"?

Would you for your part prefer nothingness?

To being, non-being?

To creativity, death?

Does the plan frighten you?

Don't you prefer it to the void of fantasy?

Evil frightens you? Don't you prefer it to indifference?

You can't put up with the wicked. Where will you go for the righteous?

You're so scared of making mistakes. How about your freedom of choice?

I offer you the opportunity of choice as an expression of freedom and love and, at the maturest moment of creation — I mean the Incarnation — I asked the most terrible choice of my Son Jesus that he could make: to die for love.

I have repeatedly told the human race, "*I set before you a blessing and a curse: choose*" (Deut 11:26).

And again, "*I have set before you life and good, death and evil: choose*" (Deut 30:15).

My decision wasn't lightly taken and I have staked everything on the choice being made.

You complain and are appalled by evil.
Why do you commit it?
Injustice revolts you.
Why do you wallow in it?
You don't like living in hatred.
Why don't you try what love can do?
Violence offends you.
Why do you choose it?
You can't put up with dirt.
Why don't you get rid of it?
Have I ever told you to do evil to yourself?
Haven't I always urged you to choose what is good?
Have I ever let you lack my "Word" to guide you?
Have I ever left you in doubt over the choices to be made?
Have I ever addressed you violently without alerting you to the prospect of peace?
Well, then!
You've thrown these two books in my face about the atrocities committed in China and Kampuchea, but have you asked yourself where the guilt lies?
Where does the root of such evil lie and how is it possible to reach such depths?
Perhaps Chinese wisdom and Kampuchean virtue weren't there to sustain people with such marvellous and illustrious traditions in their choices?
Yes, just so.
I omitted to tell you, *"that the wickedness of man was great on the earth and that every design conceived in his head was nothing if not evil"* (Gen 6:5), and to add for good measure that *"I was sorry that I had made man on earth and it grieved me to my heart"* (Gen 6:7).
Just so.
In spite of this I have to say my regret was

only relative, since *"Noah found favour in my eyes"* (Gen 6:8).

The sight of Noah standing before me even makes me forget my regret over having created him.

On the contrary, I'm glad I did.

You see, Noah's a human being, and human beings are, though sinks of corruption, capable of doing extraordinary things.

Yes, human beings find favour in my eyes.

I admit it.

I like human beings.

Human beings are my children and know their way home.

And there I am, waiting for them.

Isn't all this splendid?

Human beings are my children and I, as their father, have to train them.

What sort of training would I be giving them if I didn't allow them freedom of choice?

What virtue would be theirs, if virtue were compulsory?

If the possibility of evil-doing didn't exist and human beings were confronted only by good, what choice would there be for them to make?

What sort of love would be theirs if they were forced to love?

This is where the whole problem lies: in freedom. And among the innumerable choices I could have made when creating the human race, I preferred that of freedom, even though that choice has cost us dear.

Only in freedom can human beings become really and truly themselves.

Only in freedom are they capable of great things.

I can't abide indecisive, "lukewarm" people. In the Book of Revelation I say I find them so unbearable that I want to spew them out of my mouth (Rev 3:16).

It's not very nice, but that's how it is.

The clash between good and evil obliges my children, my human ones, to make their choices, to resolve problems, to free themselves from the torment of doubt, to demonstrate the genuineness of their love for me, who am the Absolute, who am the Truth.

Not for nothing in the Exodus did I lead them into the desert.

I wanted to find out what was in their hearts; I wanted to uncover the hidden things and I wanted them to give me a definite Yes or No. For only thus can human beings set themselves free from their vacillating, from their uncertainties, from their continual *murmurings*.

Remember: where murmuring reigns, *bliss* cannot reign, that is, the divine ability to be happy with God.

Do you follow me?

You human beings are so frightened of freedom, you don't realise it's the greatest gift I've given you.

Greater than life itself.

Life wouldn't be worth living, if it weren't for the gift of freedom.

Freedom is the *locus* of your dignity, the pledge of your virtue, the force of your love.

Could you love if you were not free?

Could you demonstrate the sincerity of your actions and thoughts if you hadn't received the gift of freedom?

So why such fear of living in freedom, costly as this may be?

I led you into the desert precisely so that you would learn to be free, to forget your conditioning and, what's more, your nostalgia for sin, so easily indulged in in Egypt and the true cause of your slavery, and of your continual wavering between Yes and No.

No, I don't care for wavering.

I don't care for it in anyone and I particularly dislike it in my child.

I want my child to be sincere, genuine, brave and loyal.

And this is why I have allowed you your freedom, even if the price of your freedom were to prove so great as to turn the universe upside down.

No, I shall never constrain my children.

I may be ashamed of them.

Though I have told them they have to make a choice, I have left them freedom of choice.

I play fair, you see!

I have given them the possibility of the kingdom and left the anti-kingdom at their elbow.

I have invited them into my Paradise and left them free to go to Hell.

Always fearful — and this is your weakness — you human beings are forever wondering whether Hell exists or not.

How can it not exist when you actually have the power of saying No to Paradise?

And what sort of paradise would Paradise be if going to Paradise were compulsory?

The choices I offer fill you with dread, yet they are genuine ones and you ought to get used to them.

Above all, you ought to get used to that freedom which is truth and the only thing that can make the facts clear to you.

Freedom is your opportunity for showing me you love me.

If you were not free, you would never be able to convince me how strongly and dearly you love me and there would always be an element of the equivocal in the relationship between God and humanity.

Freedom destroys the equivocal and makes you true to yourselves before the Absolute.

The first commandment says, "*You shall love God with all your heart, and with all your soul, and with all your might*" (Deut 6:5).

Without freedom, how could you demonstrate, how put into practice this terrible commandment?

Slavery, essentially the absence of freedom, was the point of departure for the Exodus; I, your God, commanded Moses to bring you out of Egypt so that you would learn to be free.

I know you didn't enjoy the desert, I know there was nothing there, but I also know it was the ideal climate in which to learn the value of freedom.

The desert was your place of purification.

And there it was you learned to know whether you truly loved God or preferred your personal comfort and pleasures.

In the desert you became free and able to dream of a country in which you could live safely as free agents; the Promised Land was promised precisely to ensure your freedom.

Are you still appalled by evil filling the earth?

Haven't you realised it's the obligatory *locus* of your freedom, of your choices?

I know this is a mysterious, a hard, a sometimes tragic, fact.

But it must be so.

Were it not for this dark spot, the whole of creation would go dark.


In a word, you must get one fundamental fact clear.

What fills you with repugnance, makes you suffer, makes you weep, isn't necessarily evil.

Evil is a moral quality: evil is selfishness, sensuality, pride, fear, lack of faith, non-hope, hate.

Physical pain, illness, extremes of climate whether cold or hot, old age, physical death, are natural things which can certainly make you suffer, but they aren't evil. So . . .

What sort of a world should I have created if it had no contrasting seasons, no pain, no death?

I made it as it is because I wanted it as it is.

There's no better teacher than pain, and the world would be a lifeless place were we not obliged to fulfil ourselves by means of fire and water, light and darkness, birth and death.

And it is precisely through the innumerable agonies of the created world that the visible and invisible come to fruition.

What doctor could you have without the patient, and what sort of day of rest would you have if it were not for hard work?.

I know physical death fills you with terror but I also know that the kingdom will recompense you many times over for your few moments of fear.


Have faith, humankind, I am your God; I have loved you from eternity and in me there is no deceit; if I tell you you are *good*, believe it.

For it is so.

# Human beings, my children

When I began revealing the nature of the relationship that exists between me and you, I taught you to say, "*Our Father who art in heaven.*"

It was lovely; while you were repeating "*Our Father who art in heaven*", I for my part was whispering, "*My children who are on earth*".

You said "*Father*" to me, and I said "*Children*" to you.

And that is what the bond is, honestly and truly.

I hope you don't take it merely for a compliment, a sort of figure of speech.

It is a fact.

I am your Father and you are my Children.

In every sense of the word.

I admit it may take a little while to believe these things in every particular.

You have too many theologians knocking about and far too few mystics.

Theologians are always a bit tiresome, a bit too keen on maintaining the balance.

They are hardly ever poets.

They find it an alarming idea that some funny old Christian or other can seriously believe that God, God himself, is his father, his "daddy", his very own "daddy", and they begin holding forth about the nature . . . about participation in the divine life, in so complicated a manner that eventually this "daddy" who in his own words has defined himself as "daddy" recedes further and further into the heavens, leaving the impression behind that it was all a figure of speech, a kind of compliment God uttered in a moment of inattention or sentimentality.

Perhaps all this arises from the theologians' keenness to safeguard humility — some humility! — but the sad fact is that in the ultimate analysis very few of you are convinced that I really am your father, and you treat me as though you were strangers rather than children.

It is so, believe it . . . At least that's how it seems to me.


Yes, human beings, you are my children.

Don't be afraid of repeating it, of whispering it while you're walking about or resting, when you're working and when you're praying, when you're at home and when you're out and about.

God is your father.

You are his child.

This sums up all the revelations in the Bible and is the real ''good news'' I commanded my witness and first-born son Jesus to tell you.

Everything said previously was only by way of preparation; the fullness of truth however was contained in the father-child relationship I established between myself and the human race.

Now, this is fundamental and very far-reaching.

It may even give offence to some people.

But I've never been afraid of giving offence.

I've always wanted to state the truth.

I know: there are religious people, especially in the Moslem world, who would never say that God is a father or that he could have had a child.

The relationship they postulate between God and the human race is so utterly remote as only to inspire dread, and is certainly not capable of generating loving-kindness.

30

In any case, I'm not a God "in isolation".

How could a sort of absolute monarch, shut up in his unattainable, incommunicable transcendence, think of the human race as his child? In the fullness of time I decided to reveal to the world that I was a father, that I was love, that I was communication, embrace, kingdom.

And to the human race I sent my first-born son Jesus to explain this and tell everyone about God's loving kindness, God's inner life, implicit in the great fact — for human beings — of being God's children.

Jesus is the first, but not the only one.

After him, with him, in him, many, many of his brothers and sisters will be chosen to experience this most sweet, loving, life-giving, true, luminous, fruitful, peaceful, joyous relationship which I have established between myself and the human race.

Human beings, you really and truly are my children.

Don't imagine that your destiny is confined within the narrow bounds of Earth where I have caused you to be born, where you are to take the first steps of your journey, and where I shall treat you to the first seeds of life.

The earthly experience will soon be over, as well you know, and the kingdom which is my home and is eternal will be waiting for you.

What you live on earth is merely a beginning, a childish bout of tears, an opening of your eyes to the light, a first experience of love, a test of loyalty, a school of signs, a first divine alphabet, a message of light, a mental journey, an ever stronger attraction towards the father, a search for the treasure hidden in the earthly field where you have been born into life.

But the greater part is yet to come.

Children, if you only knew what lies in store for you!

First, the eternal — for restraints and limitations will be abolished.

Then, happiness — for blood and tears will be no more.

And your food will be the contemplation of my face and love will be your fulfilment.

Then you will understand that I am your God and that you are my children.


The first thing to be born and to develop in this father-child relationship is trust, and this is fundamental since it eliminates fear.

Fear, or better, awe, is the beginning of wisdom, but gradually with maturity awe yields place to love, and this is certainly a superior stage in the relationship.

Often enough during those centuries preceding the complete revelation, my Spirit suggested wondrous words to you and, praying thus, you prayed indeed:

*"I love thee, O Lord, my strength. The Lord is my rock and my fortress, my God, my rock in whom I take refuge, my shield, and the horn of my salvation, my stronghold"* (Ps 18:1–2) and again:

*"The Lord is my shepherd, I shall not want; he makes me lie down in green pastures. He leads me beside still waters; he restores my soul. He leads me in paths of righteousness for his name's sake"* (Ps 23:1–3) and again insistently:

*"The Lord is my light and my salvation; whom shall I fear?"* (Ps 27:1) and vehemently:

*"I waited patiently for the Lord; he inclined to me and heard my cry. He drew me up from the desolate pit"* (Ps 40:1–2) and exultantly:

*"As a hart longs for flowing streams, so longs my soul for thee, O God. My soul thirsts for God, for the living God. When shall I come and behold the face of God!"* (Ps 42:1–2), and in moments of trial:

*"For God alone my souls waits in silence; from him comes my salvation. He only is my rock and my salvation, my fortress; I shall not be greatly moved"* (Ps 62:1–2), and at the first intuition of the coming kingdom:

*"How lovely is thy dwelling place, O Lord of hosts! my soul longs, yea, faints for the courts of the Lord"* (Ps 84:1–2), and joyously:

*"The Lord is my strength and my song; he has become my salvation"* (Ps 118:14), and yearningly:

*"My soul languishes for thy salvation; I hope in thy word. My eyes fail with watching for thy promise; I ask, 'When will you comfort me!' "* (Ps 119:81–82), and as fulfilment drew nearer, so the final reality became clearer:

*"Lord, my heart is not lifted up, my eyes are not raised too high; I do not occupy myself with things too great and too marvellous for me. But I have calmed and quieted my soul, like a child quieted at its mother's breast; like a child quieted is my soul"* (Ps 131:1–2).

Yes, gradually my Spirit prepared you for the complete revelation which Jesus was to sum up in the prayer "Our Father".

I hope you aren't offended by my calling you my children and won't hold it against me that I didn't ask your permission beforehand.

It's true, I didn't ask your permission, but I've given you every opportunity freely to deny that I am your father and that you are my children.

Yes, indeed . . .

And indeed there are very few of you who gladly and spontaneously accept my fatherhood.

The majority are content to exclaim, "Is that possible?" and maintain a dry and empty indifference.

It's certainly a sad sort of life, the life led by those who think of themselves as orphans, alone and, what's more, at the mercy of that fearsome environment which is the world around them.

Everything becomes a problem, a cause of darkness, pains and fear.

Above all, fear.

How are such weak, defenceless and, above all, lonely people not to live in fear?

Let's put it bluntly: anyone who doesn't discover what it is to be a child of God, to have the Creator of heaven and earth on one's side, to be sustained, guided, strengthened, justified by the Divine Absolute, lives a very sad life of it, is lit by a very feeble light, is strengthened by a truly poor hope.

Many people believe in God.

*It's very hard not to believe in him!*

But they end up stuck with an immature faith, an infantile concept of God, beset with complexes about Hell and unable to develop what really matters: that is charity, prayer, joy.

And that's all very sad.

What I've been telling you sums everything up: "I am your father and you are my children."

In the light of this, faith becomes mature, hope grows from day to day and love becomes real and strong.

God is no longer a stranger, a vague cloud, a cultural category, a conundrum.

He's a father.

And a father who creates, loves, sustains, speaks, listens, gives.

But even that's not enough.

There's more to come.

Between Father and child there's not only confidence, there's "being".

There's not only trust, there's "truth".

There's not only joy, there's "love".

When I your God try to explain to you in human terms what the nature of the divine life is, veiled in that great mystery which is God, I tell you that I am a Trinity, and it was as a Trinity that I revealed myself to you in the fullness of time.

The Father is Truth.

The Son is Truth.

The Spirit is Love.

And you too are being, truth, and love.

For the time being, you are in a state of becoming; tomorrow you will be in the kingdom in completeness.

It's because you are *being* that you are eternal and the life in you can never diminish.

It's because you are *truth* that you have to follow the truth which is Jesus.

It's because you are *love* that you can't do anything now except love.

Being gives you consistency, truth gives you the way, love gives you the eternal task.


Your task, your nature, your purpose is to love.

And this is why, since I am Love, you have to be love.

Human nature, like the Divine Nature, is love.

That is why I your God said that human beings were good.

I knew what was in them; I knew who they were.

I knew that the victory of good over evil was a certainty.

You could put your money on the human race.

I your God have put my money on you.

# Child, don't do evil

Child, we've begun to talk confidentially like old friends.

You've asked me why I have faith in human nature and what my reasons were for affirming that creation was good.

You see, child, everything is governed by the fact of my fatherhood.

If I am a father, everything becomes clear, but if you regard me as a robot or an unmoving mover or an electronic calculator or an alien, however powerful, everything stays obscure.

I have told you I am a father and you are my children.

Being a father is something quite unique, involving really extraordinary things.

Fatherhood is heaven's great experience, which they call love up here, and it's an earthly experience as well, which you call love down there.

God is defined as Love.

The Father is Love.

The creation is a work of love.

Keeping it going is a work of love.

The birth of a child is an act of love.

Relationship, dialogue is love.

God's kingdom is a kingdom of love.

I God your God am love. I created through love. I live by love.

I do nothing except for love.

And it's because I am Love that I cannot and do not know how to do evil.

And this is why I don't want my child to do it either.

It's obvious!


There are things that may be done and others that may not be done.

Evil is what may not be done.

It's obvious that you shouldn't kill.

It's obvious that you shouldn't steal.

It's obvious that you shouldn't betray.

It's obvious that you shouldn't behave violently.

There is no excuse for lying.

And there's no excuse for stealing your brother's wife.

If drugs kill, you shouldn't take them; if a sexual relationship involves deceit, you shouldn't go on with it.

Everything is straightforward for those who are straightforward; truth alone should govern your behaviour.

Stand in the truth and all will be made clear: you must not do evil.

Evil may attract you, may tempt you, but you can master it.

It is at your door, but it is bound.

Binding it depends on you.

Don't say: I don't know how to do it; that's not true.

Solemnly, long ago on Mount Sinai, I announced these things to the human race and I even wrote them in stone.

But this was only a sign.

Woe betide you if you had said "only" at the time!

How would distant — and they were the majority — or isolated peoples have got to know these things: peoples who would have to wait for centuries before seeing the arrival of a missionary?

Those who still haven't seen a missionary even today?

No, it was too important a matter to leave unresolved: every individual had the right to have an inner light to guide him or her, a sacred place in which to encounter me, the Father.

This inner light, this sacred place, is conscience: the wonder of the human race.

Conscience is the ground where Abraham encounters his God, who gives the command, "*Leave your homeland*" (Gen 12:1); conscience is Jacob's ladder joining heaven and earth.

Conscience is the place where Mary finds the courage to say Yes to the angel.

Conscience is the desert where Jesus overcomes his temptations.

Don't say: I don't know what to do.

Listen in silence to your conscience, then you'll know what!

If you wrong your fellow-being, don't forgive yourself too readily.

You shouldn't do it.

Any more than you should do what is contrary to your own human dignity.

There's nothing praiseworthy about belonging to the Mafia and it's not good to demand protection money from your fellow citizens and so deprive them of the fruits of their labour.

Cold-shoulder anyone offering you a bribe to commit unlawful acts and don't accord approval to a society governed by injustice, theft and violence.

Don't throw stones at street-lamps, don't torture dogs for fun and don't destroy what little greenery still survives the dryness of our city streets.

Don't foul the sea with dangerous, toxic waste and don't build installations that pollute the atmosphere.

Defence of the eco-system nowadays is a genuine act of charity, and respect for the environment an expression of prayer and contemplation.

The more sensitive of you have already been alerted to the risk the human race runs by destroying the environment but we're all still a long way from the goal.

Even Christians, with the weight of an authoritative message to back them, have done very little to bring home to the masses how real the environmental problems are.

All too lightly things have been allowed to take their course, the fact being overlooked that an offence against nature is an offence against creation and thus an offence against the Creator himself.

Rather than clean air to breathe and wholesome food to eat, a fistful of money has often been the determining factor.

Pollutions has now become a real danger in all sectors of life and many people are now wondering when the limit will be reached beyond which the human race cannot survive.

How carefully human beings should observe the rule long since confirmed by experience: "That which should not be done, we shall not do!"

Whatever conscience reproves you for, whatever is contrary to the common good, you should not do.

If cutting down a wood in your village diminishes the beauty of the place, don't cut it down.

Don't let yourself be corrupted by unjust administrations determining what's to be done on financial considerations alone and soliciting your support by illegal acts.

It is not good that you should sell out to the bosses; you have a duty to resist a society which thinks only of profit and power.

Hold your head high and stay clear of evil.

Your light will shine forth in the darkness.

Don't be satisfied with saying: In my country politicians are all power-mad bandits.

Try to be the opposite.

Use politics as service.

You won't be wasting your time.

Don't you know that power is the sum of all evils?

Show you aren't attached to it and you will earn the praises of the community.

Are you disgusted by what you see around you in the city?

Always do your duty and know the joy of serving your fellow-beings.

Don't forget: if you do evil, evil will do you much, much harm.

Sooner or later you will have to pay to the last penny.

There's no evading this law.

There's no escape.

For I, God, do not let evil escape.

And I pursue it wherever it may be.

I allow it no respite.

I seek it even in Hell.

For Hell is the place to which evil attempts to escape.

But there's no escape there.

If I, God, didn't know how to love, evil would succeed in its purpose, but it doesn't succeed because I am Love and between love and evil there is no peace.

Between love and evil there's war with no quarter given.

For when love conquers, evil is conquered, but when evil conquers, love is mocked.

But I don't allow love to be mocked.

When this happens I become violent — a violence to fill human beings with dread.


Doesn't death frighten you?

That's my violence.

Doesn't the lot of a drug addict or an alcoholic frighten you?

That's my violence.

Doesn't the lot of a society in ruins, or the fate of a divided family frighten you?

That's my violence.

The pain in the world, the anxiety, suffering and darkness that hold sway over human beings, are the violent sentence that I, God, enforce against the kingdom of evil.

Such is the punishment for the evil-doer; such is the hard road forcing the evil-doer to return to that very point where good was first betrayed, where disobedience first began.

There is no escape for evil.

The victory of good is inexorable, as true as God exists!

Once evil had been conceived, there was such disorder in the world that God was obliged to intervene to re-establish order.

If Cain kills Abel, Cain's path is marked out for him.

By degrees, under the Spirit of the Lord, Cain will have to repent of the wrong committed and eventually confess the truth: *"I have erred, Lord; I have done what was evil in thy sight"*.

Repentance is the first step of the return journey.

But it isn't the only one: Cain has to experience in his flesh and in his spirit that the consequences of evil will affect him forever.

The position of one having erred is not as straightforward as you may have supposed!

Christ alone, when he comes, will provide the solution for finding true peace: love.

The thrust of love is such that it asks to die of love for the sake of those whom we have caused to suffer.

On his road to liberation, Cain will reach the point where he loves Abel so much that he wants to die for him.

Not for nothing will Christ's cross, though death to him, for us become the keystone of the kingdom.

Only in the kingdom will justice and peace embrace, and evil be finally overthrown.


Children, don't do evil.

Remember you are love like me, who am your Father and am Love.

# But do good

Evil is immaturity, ignorance, weakness, darkness.

By degrees, under the action of my Spirit, you become my child; evil leaves your life, is expelled from your thoughts and no longer poisons your actions.

Holiness, which is the perfection alike of God and human beings, cannot abide evil, cannot commit it.

I who am the Holy One, your God, do not desire evil, do not do evil, do not tolerate evil.

*Holy Holy Holy* rings out in your church services and this is a praise agreeable to my heart.

Evil is liquidated by holiness, and holiness is God's life, God's joy, God's perfection.

This is why my judgement on human beings is positive.

Called to be my children, they cannot help but leave the sphere of evil to enter the reality of love, which is absolute good.

Sometimes human beings take a little while to understand, to rid themselves of their childishness, to escape from darkness, to overcome their weakness but, by degrees, sustained by my grace, which is that strength I send them day by day, they emerge victorious.

It's hard for human beings to escape my design.

I am your God.


Some of them will grasp the mystery of salvation almost immediately; others will need more time; others yet again will need to suffer much before they grasp how things work.

Remember: suffering is the instrument of your redemption, the inexorable tutor stationed at each individual's elbow.

Some in their personal desert which will come after physical death — for life goes on — will have to spend age after geological age in freeing themselves from their nostalgia for sin, in convincing themselves of the supremacy of good over evil, in recovering from deceitfulness and spite, but in the end . . .

Yes, in the end the nature of child-of-God will prevail; evil will be shut out, holiness will take up permanent residence in human nature and salvation will come, being liberation, joy and the triumph of love.

If I had to tell you the commonest reason for the delay, why protracted wandering on the paths *of Meribah and Massah in the wilderness* (Ex 17:7) is necessary, I should say it's a question of pride.

Pride is the great enemy of the human race; it is the satanic arrogance of wanting to go it alone and of not accepting the fatherhood of God, that traps human nature in its contradictions.

Lack of humility distances human beings from the truth and makes them unable to discern where the light is.

And this is what makes the road so long and the night so dark.

Believe me.

The desert in which your forefathers lived could have been crossed in fifteen days with a good camel.

It takes the proud forty years to get out of it and at what a price!

This is how pain, unpredictable circumstances, hunger, thirst become of use to the proud: they are good tools available to reality — which is God —

for teaching them what life is really about and about the irrationality of sin.

When, on the other hand, the human heart is rich in humility, what evil is in it gets circumscribed by prayer and turns into a saving cry:

*"Have mercy on me, Lord, I am a poor sinner"*
and again:

*"I lift my eyes to the hills.*
*From whence does my help come?*
*My help comes from the Lord*
*who made heaven and earth"* (Ps 121:1–2),
when the heart experiences the force of grace:

*"Those who trust in the Lord*
*are like Mount Zion,*
*which cannot be moved*
*but abides forever"* (Ps 125:1),
to sing, like Moses, having escaped from the Red Sea:

*"The Lord is my strength and my song,*
*and he has become my salvation"* (Ex 15:2).
It's then that victory becomes possible. Indeed it is said: *By praying, you save yourself.*


It's not enough not to do evil; you must do good.
I am God and have defined myself as Love.
You are my children and have to become Love.
Love is perfection for me and for you.
Love is my life and must become your life.
Love is my joy and must become your joy.
Love conquers all, achieves all, resolves all.
Try it, and you'll see.
When you're sad, do a loving deed and your sadness will pass.
When you're lonely, try to communicate with me or with your fellow-beings and loneliness will vanish.

46

When you want to experience the taste of my presence within you, do a charitable action and you will feel me.

When you feel you are dying, love; life will pulsate through you.

Love lights up all, heals all, makes sense of all.

Love is Paradise.

Who loves is in joy; who loves not is in sorrow.

Love is truth; who loves is veracious.

Love is eternal life.

The joy of the saints is to live for love.

The fulfilment of human nature is to die for love.

Where charity and love reign, there is God.

I your God have defined myself as Love.

I am Love.


The vision of evil has saddened and shocked you; compassion for human beings, especially innocent ones, has filled you with anguish.

What are we to deduce from all this?

The answer is simple: it's up to us to take action.

Things call on us; charity urges us.

You might say everything is arranged so as to engage our lives in action.

The sight of infamy, compassion for suffering humanity, the disorder we see around us, cannot leave us indifferent.

Goaded by charity and urged on by Christ himself, who has overcome evil, we launch into the task of creating a new world.

A new life lit up by love and truth begins for us today.

Here's what Francis of Assisi was saying way back in the thirteenth century:

*Lord*
*make me an instrument of your peace*

*where there is hatred, let me sow love*
*where there is injury, pardon*
*where there is discord, unity*
*where there is error, truth*
*where there is doubt, faith*
*where there is despair, hope*
*where there is darkness, light*
*and where there is sadness, joy.*

That would be no small accomplishment, and our existence would indeed blaze into a life of dazzling light.

But should we think of going a little further than Francis suggests, since the eight centuries separating us from him have accumulated more evil, more darkness, more hatred, this is what our own day suggests to us.

Have you heard of Follereau?

He was a man who devoted his life to a wonderful project for helping lepers.

He went round and round the world, founding hospitals for the treatment of leprosy and left a truly amazing achievement behind him.

Have you heard of Mother Teresa of Calcutta?

Pierced to the heart with compassion for the dying, for the derelicts of this earth, she took them into her own home; her loving example has been so powerful as to catch the imagination of the whole world.

Have you heard of the Abbé Schultz?

Thinking that his convent ought to be put to some good use, he threw its doors open and called on the young to lead a life of contemplation and struggle.

His was an epic achievement, and many rootless kids inspired by his words found new meaning in life.

Have you heard of Martin Luther King?

Exasperated by the racial injustice inflicted on blacks in the USA, he summoned everyone to non-violent struggle against evil and died a martyr for his people.

Have you heard of Bishop Romero?

He had the guts to say Mass under the muzzles of the guns of the junta oppressing his martyred homeland and to give his blood mingled with that of the sacred host, which he had consecrated and was still holding in his hands.

Have you heard of the Polish priest Popieluszko?

He pledged himself to oppose the Marxist dictatorship in his country and was beaten to death for defending Poland's freedom.

Have you heard of La Pira?

A man of our times, intelligent, courageous, rich in faith, who lived like an angel and devoted his days to work in the fields of culture and politics.

He made his activities a masterpiece of holiness.

He lived a happy man and died like a prophet.

You too must choose your field and commit yourself to the struggle against evil, against corruption, indifference and injustice.

You won't lack for somewhere to do this for it needs to be done everywhere.

Do you like teaching?

What a wonderful field for action.

Do you like social work?

There is no limit for your self-giving.

Are there too many doctors where you live?

Go and work in the developing countries.

Do you like political life?

Serve with love, distancing yourself from any thirst for power.

Do you like teaching religion?

Study the word of God and lovingly pass it on.

49

To make it easier for you to begin your task, try not to be alone; find a community that can help you.

The great Christian phenomenon of associationism is peculiar to our times.

This is truly one of those "divine moments" that sweep over the Church in difficult times — like ours — to increase the drive of the better ones among us.

Out of it has come the Scout and Guide Movement for boys and girls; out of it has come Catholic Action.

The Neo-Catechumenal Communities have come into being.

Spiritual Renewal groups have developed and every continent has seen the wonders worked by the Focolarini and the Corsillos de Cristianidad.

The parish has become the arena for the most disparate groups devoted to prayer, catechesis, and social life, as well as such movements as Notre Dame for family spirituality.

What can we say of the marvels achieved by the Base Communities in every country in the world, most particularly in those where there is a shortage of clergy, as in Brazil?

Some people, still bound to the legalism of the past, find this development somewhat frightening, seeing such communities as a danger to parochial and diocesan unity.

Some even make bold to say: "Not in this parish; I won't have it in this diocese."

This familiar clerical attitude was widespread in the past and still raises its head now and then with the words: "I prefer to have unity in my parish", which unity often means inaction, carrying on as before, services, nothing but services.

It's true that associations can cause disturbance

at first, just as it's true that no community can exist without faults.

But in the main it's the parish that isn't working properly and isn't responding to its mandate.

Indeed, how can a conglomeration of thousands and thousands of Christians held together by a few priests and organised exclusively on the basis of territory, population and Sunday worship possibly be effective?

It's painful to say this, but it's true.

Our country is widely sacramentalised but thoroughly under-evangelised.

The walk-over successes of certain foreign sects, notably Jehovah's Witnesses, are conclusive proof of this.

How are we to defend this truly endangered frontier?

We shall have to transform the parish from a supposed numerical unity into a unity composed of all kinds of association.

The parish should be the seat of all communities having anything to contribute, better still having the charisma for evangelisation, for making living, human, gospel contact with people at large.

When I was a lad, the parish that trained, educated and evangelised me wasn't the official parish, for the latter was infinitely remote from my needs; the Catholic Action group to which I belonged was what, week by week, gave me the spiritual nourishment I needed.

It's so obvious!

And if, as Jesus teaches, we ought to make a point of appraising things and institutions by their fruits, I can in all sincerity testify that virtually every serious conversion I have ever witnessed has been the result of community, as opposed to parochial, endeavour.

I have seen veritable miracles, not least those of the Neo-Catechumenal Communities who enthusiastically send married couples and priests to difficult countries, where they evangelise people living in remote districts.

And it's with joy that I say "Thank you" to all those communities working so hard as missionaries so that the young won't be alone, the parishes won't be dead and the city will resound with the sweet name of Christ.

And then always remember one thing: good never hits the headlines.

If we were to rely on the news media we should get the impression that the whole thing was on the verge of catastrophe.

We should fall prey to pessimism and our strength would desert us. But that's not how things are.

What untold good there is in the silent aspects of life!

What countless families bear silent witness to their virtue, to their commitment to the city!

What countless people live hidden lives in history!

Believe me.

# My son Jesus

Even if there had been doubt about the creation of human beings, given the gruesome pages that might be written about the world, that doubt would disappear before the beauty, the sublimity of the incarnation of Jesus.

The earth deserved to exist if only to give Jesus the chance of walking on it; the world deserved to be created if only to give him the opportunity of living and behaving as he did live and behave.

I couldn't not make the straw that was to be his cradle and I couldn't resist creating the ox and ass to keep him warm that cold night in Bethlehem.

And what could be said of the stars if among them had not been one to bear witness to the human race of the birth of the Son of God on earth?

And could I possibly, being God, have forgotten to create a mother like Mary?

What a lack of poetry in me if I had!

Just think of the woman called Mary.

Think of a creature good, pure, gentle, immaculate, who becomes heaven on earth, who generates light, who gives body and blood to Love, who has a son, who has the power of making God visible on earth, of bringing God to live among the tents of the human race, of explaining the inexplicable, of drawing the creation out of its solitude.

No, I couldn't not think of her.

The world deserved to be made, if, only for one man, called Jesus.

So I made it.

And I'm glad I did.

Jesus delights me.

*"With him I am well pleased"* (Mk 1:11).

When I created the trees, I knew I was creating one from which the wood of the cross was to be cut.

I did not hesitate to create it.

When I created thorns I knew there would be a man one day who would make a painful crown from them for my Son.

I didn't draw back.

When I created rock I foresaw the block that would be used to seal the tomb of Jesus.

I carried on.

Now, I can tell you this: as fulfilment of my son's life, nothing was more tragic than the cross but at the same time nothing more beautiful, since on this wood was consummated the greatest love a human being can have for God.

Thorns are cruel, especially when intended to convey his kingship betrayed by his fellow-beings; hard is the rock meant to shut life in the tomb forever.

But never mind.

The kingship of my Son will know a very different crown and the onrush of the resurrection will send every gravestone flying.

I want you to realise that Jesus is the explanation of all things; his life is the sum of all things.

He is the unique exemplar, the key to all mysteries; he is the light at the heart of darkness; he is the earthly Paradise; he is the kingdom of God in the midst of you.

I told you you need the space afforded you by your freedom so as to finish building your masterpiece of love.

Well, it was the same for Jesus: the earth was the place where he was free, his incarnation the completion of the creation, the roads of Palestine his opportunity to walk free and poor in search of Israel, whom he had brought out of Egypt for the very purpose of meeting and talking to him as the prophet Hosea says:

*When Israel was a child, I loved him,*
*and out of Egypt I called my son.*
*The more I called them,*
*the more they went from me;*
*they kept sacrificing to the Baals,*
*and burning incense to idols.*
*Yet it was I who taught Ephraim to walk,*
*I took them up in my arms;*
*but they did not know that I healed them.*
*I led them with cords of compassion,*
*with the bands of love,*
*and I became to them as one*
*who eases the yoke on their jaws,*
*and I bent down to them and fed them.*

The incarnation is that space afforded by freedom, in which Jesus encounters the human race, that is, Israel.

And in this space, as he invites and incites Israel to build the masterpiece of his freedom and love, so Jesus himself pursues his course, in freedom, of constructing his own masterpiece of love, I mean the victory of good over evil, the destruction of death and the leading of the entire universe to the worship of the Father.

O blessed land that saw Jesus teach human beings the freedom of love.

O truly holy land soaked with the blood shed by God to lead all to salvation.

O land ardently desired, where Jesus encountered human nature to educate it for the kingdom.

On this soil the Son of God helped every human being to become a child of God.

On this soil the visible and invisible were united once and forever in the mystery of God's kingdom.

What would this globe be like with all the people living on it if this encounter hadn't taken place?

What would this world be like without Jesus?

No, children, without the incarnation of my beloved Son, without Jesus that is to say, you cannot make sense of creation.

Without the incarnation, the earth would still be incomplete.


If we come to the mystery of evil which you find so disturbing and offensive, a mystery you always adduce when arguing that creation oughtn't to have this dark stain at the very centre of such a tissue of beauty and light, I don't hesitate to reply that my Son Jesus overcame evil by his life, that he took flesh on earth and destroyed death by his death, which creation in its ignorance and wickedness tried to inflict on him.

That dark stain on the canvas of creation was necessary.

Were it not there, the whole canvas would have stayed obscure, unintelligible, incomplete.

This very mystery of pain and death had the function of drawing my Son down to earth to compose and live the masterpiece of the redemption.

*"It was for your salvation that I came down from heaven and became incarnate of Mary of Nazareth, your sister"*.

Yes, Jesus was prompted by compassion for the human race to approach the human race and save it.

The incarnation of Jesus, his career on earth, his words, his deeds, his thoughts, his love, were his response to the innumerable demands made on the human race and all the other creatures by creation with its mystery of suffering.

Now we come to the heart of the problem, to the Gordian knot that Jesus cut by his life and death.
What did Jesus do to conquer evil?
What did he do to destroy death?
What is the meaning of these two expressions:
To conquer evil?
To destroy death?
How can we say this if, after Jesus, the world has gone on as before, sinning and dying?
Nothing has changed since Nazareth; nothing has changed since Calvary.
The world has gone on subsisting with its crimes and massacres; the human race has continued on its way with its slaveries and tears.
What has happened, for us to be able to say, "Jesus has saved us"?
What has occurred to affirm that, after him, death was destroyed and evil conquered?
Yes, this is the problem and we have to approach it with clear heads if we are to understand and solve it.
By living the way he lived, Jesus conquered evil single-handed and by dying the way he died, he swallowed up death.
The problem is personal rather than universal.
Jesus gave the example by living as he lived, by dying as he died; he explained to us how we should act in order to conquer evil and destroy death.
Human beings, do you want to free yourselves from the evil oppressing you?
Act as Jesus did.
Human beings, do you want to destroy death which is ever clutching at you?

Die of love, as Jesus did.

To overcome the evil seeking to master us, to transform our death into an act of love, is to achieve that conquest necessary for entering the kingdom, I mean the kingdom of peace and freedom, the kingdom of justice and love.

No one can discharge this task for us.

It's true, Jesus has saved us, but he's left the hard work of saving ourselves to us.

His death has justified us all, he being the Son of God, but he hasn't brought us bodily into the kingdom; he has asked us to follow him.

Since Jesus's sacrifice, each one of us is safe, but we each have to work out our own salvation.

In this resides the dignity of the human creature: being a child in relation to the Father.

In this resides the dignity of human suffering.

In this resides freedom.

Since Jesus died of love, each of us ought to die of love.

# Don't resist evil

I've told you how Jesus conquered evil and destroyed death.

He conquered evil by overcoming the temptation to commit it; he detroyed death by injecting it with love.

In brief, faced with evil, Jesus fights and conquers it in himself; faced with death, he accepts it and transforms it into martyrdom.

By dying of love, Jesus restores peace to the human race and re-establishes harmony throughout the universe.

This may not seem very much but it is everything; most importantly, his manner of acting establishes the principle of salvation.

After him, people will go on doing evil, people will go on dying, but the law of salvation has been established.

Human beings, this is your salvation:

Destroy the evil within you; mature your martyrdom.

It will be a long road but you'll be given time enough to complete it.

If this world isn't enough for you, you will have your Purgatory, your desert; but you'll get there in the end.

You have to walk the same road as Jesus.

Farewell false idols, farewell futile power, farewell wealth, farewell bossing our brothers and sisters, farewell the works of death.

Meanwhile try to memorise this very fine song based on the gospel text (Mt 5:38–42):

*Don't resist evil*
*don't resist evil*
*don't resist evil*
*don't resist evil*

*You have heard it used to be said*
*An eye for an eye and a tooth for a tooth*
*but I say to you, but I say to you*
*Don't resist evil*
*don't resist evil*
*don't resist evil*
*don't resist evil*

*And if someone strikes you*
*on the right cheek*
*turn the other to him as well*
*You have heard it used to be said*
*You shall love your neighbour*
*and hate your enemy*

*But I say to you, but I say to you*
*Love your enemies*
*do good to those who hate you*
*pray for those who persecute you*
*bless those who malign you*

*You must be perfect*
*as your heavenly Father is perfect*
*for he is kind*
*to sinners*
*for he is kind*
*to sinners*
*for he is kind*
*to sinners*

*And if anyone would sue you*
*and take your coat*
*let him also have your cloak*

*And if anyone forces you*
*to go one mile with him*
*go with him two*

*And if anyone takes from you*
*what is yours*
*don't protest*

*Don't resist evil*
*don't resist evil*
*don't resist evil*
*don't resist evil*

*Don't resist evil*
*don't resist evil*
*don't resist evil*
*don't resist evil*

This is an amazing song but Jesus's thought running through it is more amazing still.
This is the novelty of the gospel, this is Christ's good news.
This is the victory over evil.
This is the Christian revolution.
This is the way of life Jesus points out to us.
No one ever went as far as this before.
Many religions have approached the thought of Jesus in liberating force but none has ever equalled it.
And what is so grand about all this teaching is that Jesus not only taught this as being what he believed; he lived it from beginning to end.
He offered the other cheek to violence; he allowed his coat *and* his cloak to be taken away.
He loved his enemies sufficiently to die for their sake.
We might say that with Jesus it isn't the result

that counts, but the mode of acting, thinking, being.

His message is in the way he acts, lives, speaks.

In him there is a perfect union between the one who acts and the one who speaks.

He talks about non-violence and he is non-violent.

He talks about loving one's enemies, he loves his.

He talks about respect for human beings even though they are sinners.

This is what he says about evil co-existing with good, about the wicked being mixed up with the righteous:

*The kingdom of heaven may be compared to a man who sowed good seed in his field; but while people were asleep, his enemy came and sowed weeds among the wheat, and went away.*

*So when the plants came up and bore grain, then the weeds appeared too.*

*And the servants of the householder came and said to him, "Sir, didn't you sow good seed in your field? How then has it weeds?"*

*He said to them, "An enemy has done this."*

*The servants said to him, "Then do you want us to go and gather them?"*

*But he said, "No, lest in gathering the weeds you root up the wheat along with them. Let both grow together until the harvest; and at harvest time I will tell the reapers, 'Gather the weeds first and bind them in bundles to be burned, but gather the wheat into my barn ' "* (Mt 13:24–30).

This parable of the good seed and the weeds couldn't be more apposite or straightforward in explaining to me, his child, how matters stand.

The world's a field; there's the good seed the owner sows in it; then there's the mysterious intrusion of the weeds, put in by the enemy — evil.

The seed grows, and at the same time the weeds grow.

At a given moment, the problem arises: ought the weeds to be pulled up?

The owner says, No.

This decision, given so confidently by the owner, is a basic directive for the disciple.

Evil has to be left in the midst of good.

Both are to grow together until the harvest.

The servants who go to the owner proposing to suppress the wicked by force, will hear the owner reply: *"You do not know of what manner of spirit you are"* (Lk 9:55).

It is needful that evil co-exist with good; then comes the end.

It will have the honour of being uprooted before the grain, of being done up in bundles for the fire — which will burn it to ashes.

The good grain will have the last word.

This is incontestably what Jesus thought.

There's no point in resisting evil: evil reduces itself to ashes, has no future.

That is the logic of the creation; it's the logic of the One who said of it: *"It was good."*

Evil punishes itself; it self-destructs.

For human beings, for disciples of Jesus, the task is to be patient, to believe, to hope, to love.

And the victorious saying of Jesus will go on resounding through the centuries: *"If anyone strikes you on the right cheek, turn the other to him as well."*

That's the way to conquer evil. That was Jesus's way.

# Compassion

One of you earthlings has written:
  *"Everything is evil.*
  *"That is to say, everything that is is evil;*
*everything that exists is an evil and ordained to evil;*
*the purpose of the universe is evil; order and the*
*state, the laws, the ordering of nature, the natural*
*process of the universe, are not otherwise than evil,*
*nor directed to any other end than evil.*
  *"There is no good but non-existence . . ."* (from
*Zibaldone* by Giacomo Leopardi, 1474).
  I don't know what to make of him.
  Let's be content merely with saying he's a bit on
the pessimistic side.
  He sees everything as black.
  To say there's no good except *"non-existence"*
is to say the very opposite of what I myself said on
seeing the birth of heaven and earth, *"that it was*
*good"*.
  Patience!
  Everyone has the right to say what he thinks.
  I myself set the rule of freedom above all others.
  I can only add: Human beings, you're rather im-
patient creatures!
  You've no sense of contemplation.
  To prefer non-existence to existence, death to life
. . . surely that's very strange?!
  And all because you see there's suffering!
  How is it you can't manage to grasp the daily
rhythm of the natural world?
  That a blackbird should swallow a worm in a
single mouthful, that a cat should dine off a mouse,
that a fish should die in a pond, that a shepherd

should prepare a meal for his family by slitting a lamb's throat with his knife: all this you find disturbing, offensive, embittering, and perhaps it makes you think, with the author quoted above:

"*Not the individual alone but the human race entire was and will be ever, of necessity, unhappy.*

"*Not the human race alone but all the animals.*

"*Not the animals alone but all the other beings in their fashion.*

"*Not the individuals but the species, the genera, kingdoms, spheres, systems, worlds*" (*Zibaldone*, 4175).

You're in a hurry, children.

You've no sense of contemplation and poetry; you want to understand everything at once and, more particularly, you don't have a shred of faith in me.

This is wrong of you and I might describe you as proud, conceited brats.

The sight of earth and sky, contemplation of the grandeur of creation, awareness of the beauty of things, should at least leave you stunned with amazement.

Do I or don't I deserve a little trust from you?

You who are nothing, nothing, nothing, who have made nothing out of nothing, might at least stand in silent awe before creation.

But, no . . . you immediately want to pass judgement . . . to condemn. Naturally, there are some things you can't understand that astound you and, not to put too fine a point upon it, offend you.

Yet, couldn't you ask yourselves with a grain of humility: doesn't the One who made the world we know, who placed the mountains and spread out the surface of the seas, who made room for the galaxies and created the atom, deserve a little trust?

I want to trust the Spirit that created the visible and the invisible.

I shall expect him to understand but shall give him the right to be heard to the end of his discourse.

I shan't interrupt him at the very beginning by saying, "You're cruel, you allow the dragonfly to be eaten by the cockchafer!"

What, pray, do you know about dragonflies?

Or what happens when they die?

Yes, what happens when the gazelle expires in the desert after running for miles to escape the jackal?

What happens when a flower withers?

When the lamb enters its death agony under the butcher's knife?

What do you know about it?

What if, at that moment, there were high festival?

What if pain turned into joy?

What if death became life, more life, all life?

This is the only mystery I have left you with in creation; why do you take it so amiss?

It was certainly a cruel thing for human beings to have crucified Jesus and you might well reproach God for having stayed silent over the tragedy of Calvary, and yet . . . Have you experienced the resurrection?

Have you made the transit from the visible to the invisible, to see what happens?

Certainly, if everything ended with death whether for the dragonfly or for the grass of the field or for my son Jesus, you would be right, but . . .

It isn't like that.

Life goes on.

It not only goes on, it develops, grows, matures.

Life is eternal and you haven't seen the best of it: the kingdom.

The discourse of the earth and sky is only the beginning of our discourses.

There are others I've prepared for you, which you'll hear on the other side of physical death.

And that's when you'll say joyfully, "Now I know; God is truly God."

If you were really humble, you would be able to say this already and it would be the strength of your life and the joy of your contemplation, but . . . this requires patience from me too who am your God!

In any case let's have no more whining over the death of insects or the nasty habit of eating meat.

Even Jesus, my son, ate lamb that Passover evening.

And don't forget: it was he who conquered death.


There is, I think, some justification for your pangs over the misery that fills the world and the pity you feel for the sufferings of the innocent.

Especially for your pangs over the sufferings of the innocent.

However, we may as well say, the grass is innocent when it's mown; the swallow too is innocent when it dies in a storm while flying to its nest; people are often innocent who catch fatal diseases.

It is true, the best suffer the most, those sensitive souls who weep over the world's misery.

You have written books and books instinct with fine feelings on this topic; you have talked and talked about the sorrows of the innocent.

It must however be said that your sorrowing hasn't always been very heart-felt.

Many of you talk about suffering but won't lift a finger when it comes to relieving the sufferings of the poor.

And what about the sentimental attitude to the death of insects?

You don't hesitate over spraying all the trees in your orchards, causing a general massacre of insects, and you don't feel at all concerned about soaking the soil with weed-killers to get rid of what you've dubbed parasites.

In such matters you wouldn't hesitate to suit your own convenience.

Yet you pause to grizzle over a spider that, weaving its wondrous web between two flowery boughs, has caught a fly to eat and so absorb a little protein.

Even so, the fact of compassion remains; this does you honour and indicates delicacy of soul.

I've heard it said by one of you, "Compassion is greater than God, especially a God I don't know."

I agree! I know what this feeling in the human heart is worth!

If I had to reveal a fraction of the mystery to you, I should tell you I've designed all sorts of things with a view to arousing the emotion of compassion in you.

Only think!

If compassion for children dying of hunger, for skeletal mothers with no milk for their babies, were to prompt the Christians of America, England, Italy to rush to the aid of poor countries and send even the superfluity of their wealth to feed them!

If compassion for men with no work and no means of fulfilling themselves because they are being crushed by an all-powerful, all-planning, all-selfish society, were to prompt rulers and politicians to act in such manner as to transform the wealth of states into work for all!

If compassion for boys and girls who destroy themselves with drugs by becoming slaves to a pleasure that kills, were to prompt states to burn the fields where the terrible poison is grown and replace this crop with products useful and good! At once you say, the world would change for the better.

Well, I admit to you: I created physical pain to shake you out of your inertia and I sowed compassion in the world to prompt you to come to the defence of the innocent and the poor.

Compassion is a feeling that does you honour and well you know the energy it can release in the human heart.

Many, many people act and strive under the goad of compassion.

Many transform their lives into masterpieces of light and love, goaded by anguish generated by compassion for the sick, the weak, the poor, the innocent.

Yes, compassion can help you, can give you poetry and sweetness, can fill your days with fruitful, creative activity, can renew your life, can correct your pride and overcome your egoism.

Of my son Jesus the gospel has recorded, *"When he saw the crowd, he had compassion on them, because they were tired, worn out like sheep without a shepherd"* (cf. Mk 6:34).

How wonderful the compassion of Jesus!

# Intimacy with God

If it rains, if the wind blows, if drought damages your harvest, if winter lasts longer than usual, if the clouds hide the stars just above your house, what can you do about it?

Can you control the rain, stop the wind, overcome the drought, shorten the winter, disperse the bothersome clouds so that you can gaze at the stars?

Of course not.

Faced with things too strong to cope with, there's nothing for it but to watch, think and wait.

Can you impose a design on your surroundings, these being so important to you, given that harvest, health and life depend on them?

Climbing upwards and outwards, can you reposition a galaxy, halt a comet, fix the temperature of a star?

Going further still, can you reach the limits of the universe, enter the black holes in space and see if there are other universes, other worlds, other vastnesses beyond?

Well?

You have to admit to being surrounded by the most absolute, most impenetrable, most transcendent mystery.

The same thing happens if you invert the process and turn your attention from the extremely large to the minutely small.

That's how it is, whether you like it or not.

So why get upset?

When I look at you I get the feeling that you are convinced you can alter things, and that you regard yourselves as being in charge.

Some of you give the impression of being God yourselves or nearly so, reducing God to a little cloud incapable of thinking, of planning projects, of willing the order of things.

Think about this.

If you were children, proper children, then instead of bothering your heads about what you can't do, you would be silently contemplating things, making a habit of looking at the world, nature, history, the heavens, with ecstatic eye, without tension, without futile demands, without fear, singing Alleluja before what gives you pleasure and keeping quiet, incurious and patient before what you find disturbing.

Can I, your Creator, ask you for a little trust?

It shouldn't be so hard when everything bears witness to me.

Think how lovely it would be to see the human race in contemplation of the visible world, forever oscillating between "A joyful Alleluia" and, when mystery tests their mettle, a "Father, I surrender myself to you".

In fact praying begins with the word "Thanks" and ends with the words that Jesus taught you, "Thy will be done".

Anything else is unworthy of the Love I am.


Intimacy with God begins and ends with trust.

I love the human race so much: *Those who trust in the Lord.*

Of them I have said: *They cannot be moved but will abide forever.*

I urge you to try.

You can't have more absolute joy!

Life will become Paradise, intimacy, continual prayer.

Try saying:

*"I love thee, O Lord my strength.*

*The Lord is my rock, my fortress and my deliverer; my God, my rock, in whom I take refuge"* (Ps 18:1–2).

I'm your Father; it shouldn't be hard.

It shouldn't be hard to believe that God created heaven and earth, that he governs all things and that he will lead everything to its fulfilment.

It shouldn't be hard to feel me as being very close, *"like someone who lifts his infant to his cheek to kiss it"* (cf. Hos 11:4).

It shouldn't be hard to convince yourselves that your story and my story are intertwined like love stories.

If you set store by your life, your holiness, your salvation, how much more do I set store by these things, who am your Father!

Surrender yourselves to me, my children; believe in me.

Your days should be one unending quest for intimacy. *"All who are mine are thine,"* Jesus told me (John 17:10).

To whom I found it easy to reply: *"And all those who are mine are thine"*.

As though that were not enough, he prayed as follows:

*"Thou in me and I in thee, that we may be perfectly united"* (cf. John 17:23).

Try it and you'll see.

The life of intimacy led in the here-and-now anticipates the kingdom and is true peace.

Here are one or two words of advice. Write: When you get up in the morning, open the window and pray: My God, I love you.

When you're at work and get tired and feel a need

72

for help, peacefully say: Father, I surrender myself to you.

When you find yourself in conflict with history or your fellow beings, pray as follows: Thy kingdom come, thy will be done.

When you are in pain, bearing the passion of Jesus within you, firmly say: Thy will be done, O Lord.

When everything in life looks black and you can't manage to grasp the threads of God's presence within you, boldly say: Lord, thou art my shepherd.

When you are near death, celebrate your Mass, look at my Son on the cross and say your Amen.

At that moment you won't be alone; I shall be with you as I have been all your life.

Remember: this is when true life begins.

PART TWO

# HUMAN BEINGS,
# WHAT HAVE YOU TO SAY?

# The parable of the prodigal son

I'm a young man who lived in Palestine before the coming of Jesus. I was the restless type, easily influenced by bad company.

I disliked my elder brother; he seemed to be on my back all the time, ready to discipline me or put me to work.

I found living at home very irksome and was continually aware of not being able to get on with my father.

I was constantly wrangling with my father and brother and grew more and more determined to run away.

I convinced myself I should find happiness elsewhere and I made this more and more obvious.

Life became unbearable and one day my father said to me, "My boy, if you don't like it here with us, go where you please. The world is wide."

So I left home, with the help of a money present which my father in his generosity would not let me leave without.

The first stop on my escape was the city not far from the town where I had always lived.

There I made new friends who had the same lifestyle as myself and for a while we lived well enough with the help of the money my father had given me.

This state of affairs didn't last long, since life is full of problems if you don't have any ideals.

My money ran out and so did my friends.

I began feeling lonely and became aware of a sort of inner anguish, coupled with a sadness I had hardly known before.

I felt frightened too but paralysed by the situation.

I started working somewhat half-heartedly, a bit here, a bit there, but without any great result.

What a strange place the world is! When you're cheerful and have money in your pocket, it smiles on you, but when you're sad and broke, it deserts you.

It wasn't long before I felt deserted.

I passed my time gambling, drinking and whoring, but things went from bad to worse for me.

My heart grew hard and my money, what little I managed to win, I spent on fornicating with the most degraded women around.

To the misery in which I was living was soon added another that admitted no escape: famine, which devastated the area and made life difficult for everyone.

It was no laughing matter.

I couldn't get enough to eat any more.

Old friends began to shun me, for they had their problems too. Everyone had problems. Having tried everything I could think of, I had recourse to an old friend of my father's, though not without some misgiving on the score of my self-esteem.

He received me kindly enough and, in view of the long-standing friendship, suggested I should go and look after a herd of pigs some distance away in an inaccessible, fairly disagreeable place.

I was in no position to refuse and soon found myself amid woods and precipices looking after animals which were certainly happier than I was, particularly since they were gorging themselves on big carob-beans in which the district abounded.

I had only ever eaten carobs for fun as a boy with my mates, picking the best fruit on the trees.

I could have managed on that, since carobs are nourishing and sweet.

However . . .

The famine got so bad that I had to help some of the servants pick the fruit to store for the winter.

Things couldn't have been worse. With the harvest in, my last chance of eating as much as I wanted disappeared.

I wandered among the clumps of trees looking for the left-overs from the harvest but the boss's pigs, being much cleverer than I was, had made a clean sweep of the carobs.

There was nothing left, absolutely nothing.

Things were really bad, and if I ever went near the sacks of carobs in the stores, I could see the servants' expressions grow grim and hostile.

Leave them alone, you good-for-nothing, those acorns are for the animals, not for you.

Go and fend for yourself.

Fend for yourself is excellent advice, but how do you do it in a famine-stricken land?

My stomach ached for days on end, on account of the emptiness to which it was subjected.

I ate grubs: I ate anything that came to hand until I reached the point where I would grab a few carobs from the pigs at the risk of getting bitten.

It couldn't go on like this; I was reduced to tears as I sat under the huge oak trees.

When things were at their worst, I began remembering my home, my father.

I saw the threshing-floor where the grain was winnowed from the chaff, the fields with their ripe crops, my father's servants sitting down at midday to a lunch of bread and meat.

How differently things looked at that distance, in my thoughts!

What could I have been thinking about to have left such a marvellous place, to fall into such a hell-hole of drought, hunger and loneliness?

I hadn't understood. That was it, I hadn't understood.

My father's smile had made me fed-up. Now I enjoyed the smile of bitter solitude.

I had needed to go through all this to realise the truth.

How could I have learnt it except in the school of hardship?

I saw things differently now and realised where I'd gone wrong. I'd needed to learn in the harsh school of evil, disorder, prostitution, irrationality.

I'd been obstinate but, like a good teacher, evil had changed me.

Yes, now I would go home, convinced of my mistakes at last.

And home I went.

I found my father waiting for me. He had been sure I would come back.

I was bowled over by his kindness, even though I'd been well aware of it from the outset.

What celebrations we had! I enjoyed times such as I hadn't known for ages.

At night I would lie relaxed on my bed and think that the evil I'd ignorantly imbibed hadn't been useless.

For evil itself had prompted me to come home.

It struck me as odd but there it was: hunger, cold, loneliness, the harsh realities of the world had done more to bring me to my senses than had my mother's smile or my father's care.

Yes, even evil had its mission to hard hearts like mine.

The world seemed more normal to me and I began to see things the right way.

# The parable of the junkie

By way of contrast, I'm a young man of 26, born in the era of Jesus but, as we say, a child of our times.

I wanted for nothing when I was growing up, for our way of life was called *consumerism*.

I preferred sleeping to studying, playing to applying myself to my tasks.

I never even considered running away from home, since my home made the easy life I loved even easier.

The prodigal son in Jesus's parable left home to run after women.

In our case there was no need to do this as morals were such that I could get as many women as I liked and to spare.

Sex was a marketable commodity and every refinement of self-indulgence was available.

The thirst for pleasure knew no bounds; nothing is more destructive.

We knew about drugs, we were crazy for them, and used to ''shoot up'' with wild abandon.

To start with, it seemed harmless enough, but then we heard of people actually dying. People explained how dangerous it was but by then it was already too late.

Who could get free of a craving like that? How true it is that pleasure kills!

This caused a terrible crisis at home.

My mother couldn't stop crying and my father was worried out of his wits.

To wean me off drugs they tried not giving me

any more pocket money, but there were things of value in the house to pay for my fixes.

I stole everything of saleable value.

I was even cruel enough to steal things dear to my mother and sisters.

I was no longer moved by my mother's tears.

My father was terrified in case I ended up stealing outside the home.

I did become a thief and, to get money to buy drugs, I used every trick in the book.

Then there were visits from the police and my father, who was a man of exceptional rectitude, fell ill for some time as a result. He'd reached the end of his tether.

He'd seen everything go to pieces around him.

An intelligent friend of his gave him some advice, "Kick him out of the house! It's the only way of saving him. As things are, he's incapable of obeying you."

My mother was appalled at the idea.

It seemed an inconceivable thing to do. "As a mother, how can I reject my son?"

She took a great deal of convincing and it wasn't easy to reach a decision. Nonetheless it was the right one.

The smiles of my dear ones, the care they lavished on me, weren't the right school for me any more.

My father, my mother and the spick-and-span environment of home could make no further impression on me.

A friend of my mother's, who was a priest, told her one day it was absolutely essential for her to change her method of dealing with me, and he quoted her a saying of St Paul's, applicable to an individual no longer prepared to accept the Church's discipline: "*Deliver him to Satan*" (1 Cor 5:5).

And delivered to Satan I was.

They shut me out of the house, sent me away without a penny. I ended up sleeping under bridges and in railway booking-halls.

For me the world changed altogether.

It was as though the only light encouraging me to behave with a minimum of decency had been extinguished; I mean the light of home.

From now on, the world became my home and vice my clothing. I was arrested several times.

One day, in a shared prison cell, I experienced the blackest shame I had ever known. I was stripped by a group of men as wretched as myself and brutally raped.

It was probably at that moment, having reached the depths of misery, that I resolved to escape from the abyss.

I could think of no other way of saving myself than that of turning back. I would have done anything I could to escape.

But it was far from easy, especially since I was more than half convinced that this was something from which there was no escape.

I had managed to escape from my father's smiles, but I wouldn't be able to escape from the Evil One's grinning.

My father had been a poor teacher with his kid-gloved approach; Satan had made me give in.

I understood now how even evil can be of value to us in our weakness and how twenty days in gaol could be of more use than a trip to Miami.

I went home and delivered myself into the hands of my dear ones.

I said, "Tie me up, shut me up in a cell; I want to beat it."

Feeling incompetent themselves, they got help

from a detoxification centre. I went through a tough time but in the end I beat it.

Now I am free, no longer enslaved to drugs, and prepared to admit that the horror of prison-life and nights spent under the arches can be helpful to anyone who's weak and without ideals.

God can draw good out of evil. God overcomes! He allows even evil to help us along our hard road.

Yes, even the darkest darkness can spur us towards the light and bring salvation nearer.

# Apocalypse

It isn't easy to talk about justice in history.

It can only be done once love has passed by, once God by his bloody sacrifice has shed his redeeming blood on the Calvary of the world.

That blood resolves every tension, cancels every obscenity, gives innocence to every crime.

In that blood we have all been washed.

Were it not for this washing, there would be no peace for the human race for all eternity.

Peace was the very reason why Jesus died for us.

Closing the spiral of violence and revolt, Christ in himself expiates sin and overcomes its inevitable consequence, death.

Which leaves history to describe for us, chapter by chapter, century by century, what the consequences of evil are.

History is the expert on life, telling us what has happened on the human journey whenever human beings have deserted the ideal of perfection laid down in the word of God.

Let's take a single passage and read it in silence:

*Who is this that comes from Edom,*
  *in crimsoned garments from Bozrah,*
*he that is glorious in his apparel,*
  *marching in the greatness of his strength?*
*"It is I, announcing vindication,*
  *mighty to save."*
*Why is thy apparel red,*
  *and thy garments like his that treads in the*
    *wine press?*
*"I have trodden the wine press alone,*
  *and from the peoples no one was with me;*

*I trod them in my anger*
*and trampled them in my wrath;*
*their lifeblood is sprinkled upon my garments,*
*and I have stained all my raiment.*
*For the day of vengeance was in my heart,*
*and my year of redemption has come.*
*I looked, but there was no one to help;*
*I was appalled, but there was no one to uphold;*
*so my own arm brought me victory,*
*and my wrath upheld me.*
*I trod down the peoples in my anger,*
*I made them drunk in my wrath,*
*and I poured out their lifeblood on the earth.''*

This is perhaps the most terrifying passage in Isaiah (63:1–6).

This vision of someone treading the winepress of the wrath of God, disdainfully trampling on the peoples, grinding them down in wrath until he sees the ground awash with their blood and his clothes stained red, has something apocalyptic about its truly tragic grandeur.

Yet the vision is not apocalyptic; it is a vision of today and every day, and each of us has a particular way of seeing it.

Few generations have not, in the course of their history, had occasion to see peoples slaughtering one another and their soil awash with rivers of blood.

Nor is there any need to hark back to the massacres of Tamerlane and Ghengis Khan, to the pogroms of the past in which entire peoples were wiped out.

It's sufficient to relive in memory the last two world wars, the loss of life in the European trenches, the genocidal acts of World War II, the barbarities of the Nazi extermination camps, for Isaiah's prophecy to become reality.

And what about the Iraq-Iran war on the plains by the Shatt-al-Arab in the Middle East, where thousands and thousands of men have been killed, dying out of misconceived zeal to give glory to God?

No question but that, to a man of peace, analysis of such horrors will lead to a pessimistic view of human nature.

How can all this happen?

How is it possible to drench the world in blood like this, to kill, maim, beat up one's fellow-being, burn his house down, embitter his existence, sweep away all he has, including his sense of religion?

To what purpose?

For what reason?

Yes, human beings, you're delinquents, you're murderers, you're Cain and worse than Cain.

How could God, when he created you, have said of you *that you were very good*?

If you were only good at waging war . . .

But you are good at starving whole continents by robbing the poor of raw materials.

That's a subtle way of enslaving people who can't take counter-measures.

Then there's injustice and racial hatred.

There's the production and distribution of drugs to kill off the unborn.

What a spectacle!

What a horrid picture human beings present in the perspectives of history!

How can we possibly go on having faith?

How can I believe in the goodness of life, in the logic of existence?

How can I greet the new day with faith, as it dawns on my road?

It was at this point that God said to me, ''Sit

down, let's talk as father to son in simple terms. Here's the subject I'm giving you for today. Write!"

And I wrote, "We are not punished for our actions, we are punished by them, as we are rewarded by them."

How true this axiom is!

Our actions contain punishment or reward, depending on what we have done.

You wage war?

War brings you the just return of ruin, hatred, destruction.

There's no need to punish anyone who has unleashed hatred.

Hatred itself will be your reward.

You poison the air with your deadly products which in turn destroy your forests and give you leukaemia.

You give yourself over to the vice of gluttony and your vice destroys your health.

You drug yourself and your brain turns to pulp.

You take possession of a country, seizing the land from the peasantry; one day the peasantry will rebel against you and kill you.

You misuse your sexuality and turn love into a consumer service.

Don't be surprised if enraged nature takes revenge on you.

No, friends, there's no point in saying, "God is punishing you."

That's what the ancients used to say, and people in the Middle Ages.

Instead you must say, "I'm punishing myself; my own actions are punishing me."

Believe me, friends, most of the evil in the world that you find disturbing and shocking is contrived by your own hand, by your perverse attitudes of mind, by your thirst for power and by your lust for pleasure.

Don't say, "God has made a mess of things and I don't understand what he's about."

Rather say, "We are guilty people, we are the ones who turn the world into a sewer and human relationships into fratricidal wars."

I know you find that passage from Isaiah offensive and you don't know who it is that's going to come from the world of sin and slavery known as Edom to tread the winepress of the wrath of God until his clothes are spattered with blood: but I know.

One day you will see who he is, when the heavens open and the visible and invisible are united in the Apocalypse of history and the vision of the kingdom.

For the meanwhile, stay silent and if possible on your knees and, weeping, contemplate the world's expanse where brothers are shedding one another's blood, where children are dying of hunger, where the rich steal raw materials from the poor, where dictatorship, violence and torture hold sway.

Don't keep wondering whether God is the figure trampling the winepress of revenge, but live in a way that allows you to disarm, for fear of experiencing something worse.

Seek peace.

You would do much better to devote the money intended for armaments to lending a hand to peoples who are setting out on their journey and need all the help they can get, particularly understanding and sympathy.

Here it strikes me I ought to tell you something.

What I see isn't entirely evil.

From time to time I feel like presenting you with a diploma of honour.

You are such fine fellows!

When I look at your advances in technology I really am impressed.

You really are fine children!

And what you've been able to do with your technology!

By slow scientific research, by the painstaking solution of nagging problems, you have achieved truly wonderful things.

From the sun you stole the principle and force of its energy and forthwith transformed this into a bomb to kill hundreds of thousands of people at a blow.

I can call you fine children for having discovered how to enclose a piece of the sun inside a metal casing.

But I can't call you that when I see you've used it to destroy a city.

How sick your hearts are!

Admit it.

There's another marvel you've contrived to perform.

You've managed to enclose the whole world with its remotest places inside a sitting-room where you can see and hear all your fellow-beings on every continent; and then you've transformed your sitting-room into an instrument of vanity and an all too often superficial peepshow where your children learn to waste their time and grow incapable of reading a serious book.

If only you used your technology to make the world a better place, to make more food available for poor countries, to harness the forces of nature, to unite the peoples in a common effort, to overcome evil!

But instead . . .

How wicked you are!
How sick in your hearts!
So don't be surprised if from Edom, the land of
slavery, comes a punishment that soaks your
clothes in blood!

# The effort of faith

Jesus satisfied five thousand people's hunger in a lonely place overlooking the lake, his lake.

He made them sit on the grass in groups of a hundred and groups of fifty and, with five loaves and two fish, not only filled all their stomachs but twelve baskets as well with the leftovers.

The sign was very clear.

When someone can feed so many people in the wilderness, God is clearly present.

God is with us.

Mark continues his catechesis, *"He made his disciples get into the boat and go before him to the other side, to Bethsaida, where he dismissed the crowd.*

*"And after he had taken leave of them, he went into the hills to pray"* (Mk 6:45–46).

Matthew follows the same line, adding at this point that Jesus was alone.

Then the picture grows wider and heaven and earth contemplate what is happening on the lake.

*"The boat was many furlongs distant from the land, beaten by the waves, for the wind was against them.*

*And in the fourth watch of the night he came to them walking on the sea.*

*But when the disciples saw him walking on the sea, they were terrified, saying, 'It is a ghost!' And they cried out for fear. But immediately he spoke to them, saying, 'Take heart, it is I; have no fear' "* (Mt 14:24–27).

Poor Jesus!

He must have felt really fed up at having to say, "Cheer up, don't be frightened, it's only me!"

We don't believe in ourselves, we're afraid, we start trembling, our eyes go out of focus and may even mistake Jesus for a ghost.

Even worse . . .

At this point, prompted by insecurity, we have no choice but to ask him for yet another sign; Peter's the one to ask him, " 'Lord, *if it is you, bid me come to you on the water.'*

*"He said, 'Come' "* (Mt 14:28–29).

Faith is the matter in hand; our faith is always so niggardly, so weak, so poor.

Now I shall throw myself out, thinks Peter.

I have no other choice.

I want to try!

And he throws himself out.

Oh, he's certainly not frightened of the lake.

He's a fisherman.

He's waded into it countless times.

A good swimmer can easily keep afloat.

But that isn't it; it isn't physical fear of the water that worries him.

He has seen Jesus walking on the water.

The test of faith won't be to swim to Jesus.

He has to walk to Jesus, who is standing there, upright, in front of him in the semi-darkness.

The water has to act as a pavement under his feet; the water has to support him upright, and this is something Peter has never experienced.

That's the proof that the chap standing over there isn't a ghost, but Jesus.

He throws himself out.

For a moment all goes well, while he doesn't analyse what's happening.

Just as Matthew says, *"He began walking on the water and went towards Jesus."*

93

We don't know how many steps he'd taken or whether he walked like a tightrope-walker with his arms outstretched to keep his balance.

What we do know is that he walked, looking at Jesus in front of him.

Then . . . then . . . then . . .

*"But when he saw how violent the wind was, he took fright and, beginning to sink, he cried out, 'Lord, save me!' "* (Mt 14:30).

How often I've heard this cry of Peter's echoing in my soul!

No, not even I, even though I'm a poor swimmer, am frightened of sinking when there's such a big boat standing by.

It isn't very hard to clamber back to one's shipmates, even if the night is dark.

What makes me cry out, what makes Peter cry out, is the mortal weakness of our faith.

Peter asked for the sign of walking on the water, not that of making a dash to Jesus, for that was easy, commonplace.

Walking on the water was a sign that God is no ghost, that Jesus is the Lord of history and of events, that he is the God of the impossible.

This is the substance of faith, the new aspect of the relationship with the divine, the confidence that God is with us, that the world has been overcome, that death has been swallowed up by Christ, that eternal life exists, that we are immortal.

This isn't easy; it is indeed the hardest effort we have to make on earth.

Believing, hoping, loving, represent the masterpiece of this mysterious tension between heaven and earth, between the visible and invisible, between a God who, for us, is a ghost and the God who, for us, is Father, Brother, Friend, Spouse.

There's one creature however who didn't cry out when confronted with the mystery, who didn't mistake the Angel Gabriel for a ghost but remained sweetly serene in the presence of the divine: Mary of Nazareth.

This isn't a compliment we wish to pay her; it's the truth.

Mary overcame the ordeal of faith.

The waters of life were just as bitter for her as they were for Peter; the sea was by no means calm for her when she was faced with the proposal that she should become the mother of God; the mystery of giving Christ a body was much more demanding than a stroll on the water; yet Mary didn't hesitate, but set off towards Jesus.

*"Blessed are you, Mary, because you believed"* (cf. Lk 1:45).

Yes, I acknowledge Mary as mistress of my faith.

Yes, how impressed I am by such serenity, such courage!

I certainly shouldn't have been able to say Yes to such a terrifying proposal that history should be fulfilled like this through me.

I should have demanded a thousand explanations and shuddered at the thought of being taken for a sinner by all the good folk living in our parish.

Don't let's forget: Mary accepted the role of teenage mother to veil the mystery of divine paternity!

*"Blessed are you, Mary, because you believed,"* the centuries will sing.

Mary walks on the waters of contradiction and doesn't mistake Jesus for a ghost, as we who are full of fear do.

Mary doesn't cry out with Peter, but prays ecstatically, saying:

*"My soul magnifies
the Lord,
and my spirit rejoices
in God my Saviour"* (Lk 1:46).


How great faith is, dear brothers and sisters!

How wonderfully hope overcomes our weakness!

What a novel experience charity is, making God manifest in us!

This is what we ought to be striving for; other things don't matter so much.

*"Lord, increase our faith"* (Lk 17:5) we ought to say, day by day, with the disciples and the father of the epileptic boy whom Jesus cured (cf. Mt 17:14–20).

*"Faith is the assurance of things hoped for.*

*"It is the conviction of things not seen,"* St Paul tells us (Heb 11:1), and nothing is more useful for us on the journey to the kingdom.

The things hoped for are holiness on this earth and the eternal kingdom after our ordeal.

The things unseen are the presence of God in us and in history.

That's all.

And with faith we have the conviction of being invincible.

With faith, poverty is overcome.

With faith, the waters become a path on which we can walk.


But what an effort!

I think that for myself, for Christians, for everyone, the common point of encounter must be faith.

The various religions have value in so far as they

train us to have faith, but faith transcends them and unites them all.

The religion of the mature human being is faith and faith is simple, even though terribly hard for everyone.

Faith means believing in God the Father Almighty, Creator of heaven and earth.

Faith means believing in Jesus Christ who saves us.

Faith means believing in eternal life.

Only a few things but fundamental ones, to ward off the temptation of the void and the loneliness that makes us cry, *"Save us, Lord, we are perishing"* (Mt 8:25).

# Second attempt

Theologians will forgive me if at this point I take the liberty of considering matters not yet precisely worked out as regards what may happen after death: only details, of course, the general principles being well known.

One thing I'm sure of: I shall never step outside the orthodox teaching of the Church.

I honestly don't feel the need to, having over the years grown progressively aware of how genuinely our mother she is.

The subject is this: if I were to die tonight, the conviction is clear in my mind: Paradise, no.

I know from experience that if God is Love — as indeed he is — the examination at life's eventide is about love.

But just because there is this exam, I feel my destination to be fair: Paradise, no.

Paradise is the place of absolute love, and is earned by an act of perfect love such as Jesus made on Calvary by dying of love.

Of which, unless something extraordinary were to occur in these closing days of my life — martyrdom, for instance — I can say with complete conviction: Carlo isn't up to it.

Your love still isn't as mature as that, as radical as that; you still don't know how to die of love.

So . . . Paradise, no.

But with just as much conviction, I say: Hell, no.

I know my God.

I've had a close and loving relationship with him for many, many years.

I truly love him, am happy in his presence, pray

to him from sunrise to sunset, and now during the night too.

He has revealed himself to me in contemplation as knowledge; I know his Word by heart.

I know his tastes.

It's because I do know his tastes that I'm sure of my salvation.

I know he wants me to be saved; he has told me so in the Bible in many different ways.

So . . . Hell, no.

Well!

If Paradise isn't to be mine yet, if Hell wasn't meant for his children, where shall I go?

Where will the angels put me, on that evening when I have to leave the earth?

I know I shall fail my exam as on a thousand other occasions, whether because of my self-centredness or because of my bad habit of thinking too much about me and not letting charity empty myself of myself.

However . . .

There must be some place where one can prepare for sitting one's exam over again, mustn't there?

I don't care for my oriental friends' notion that one will eventually be reincarnated in another creature or person, in whose borrowed body I shall have to complete my purification.

I'm sick of being here on earth and may, as a son who loves his father, ask for somewhere calmer and more metaphysical.

Yes, metaphysical like the desert.

I shall ask him for the desert; this would suit my requirements exactly.

For the desert was the place of purification for God's people.

I shall ask him for the desert.

I know the very spot, out there between Tit and

Silet, where I used to be when I was young and where, as I recall, I rolled in the burning sand with joy, shouting, "My God, I love you!"

There I shall prepare for sitting my exam again, as sooner or later I shall have to, for the desert is certainly not a place of fixed abode.

That's only up there, in the kingdom.

I humbly beg the theologians to let me use this image, this sign, that I've found very helpful throughout my life.

It's this: we are born on earth and, like a grain of wheat, set out on our road between dry soil and water.

The whole thing is a matter of potentiality in so far as, if you had to explain what a grain of wheat is and what it's doing in the sower's bag and why it's thrown into the furrow, the answers wouldn't be very easy for your listeners to understand.

We know what a grain of wheat is, swelling with life, and we know it doesn't live very long.

It dies in the furrow and from it sprouts a little green shoot.

Then the shoot grows, getting stronger, and when it reaches the height of about a metre the ear sprouts from it with thirty, forty, a hundred grains, as the parable of the sower says.

Look, this is where the theologians smirk.

The earth is the place where the grain is born and dies; the sprout is the desert of purification; the ear is the fullness of the kingdom.

I love this image, I find it comforting.

I know I shall have to die; I know that what I've done is incomplete, but I also know that I shall have the whole of time in which to mature, to review and rethink my existence.

The ear, the kingdom, isn't going to pounce on me without warning.

100

I've never found the scenario convincing of the priest racing along the motorway to get to an accident victim who's holding his guts in with both hands — to remind him about eternal life.

If God intervened in our affairs which, being eternal among other things, are therefore rather important, he would be displaying poor taste if he did so in such a curious manner.

Not even earthly judges pass sentence on the guilty without giving them time to collect their thoughts and put on a clean tie.

No, I don't care for this making use of unforeseen death to terrify sinners.

In our relationship with God there are plenty of other opportunities for getting things straight and for convincing ourselves that the Absolute has to be taken seriously.

But love has to be taken seriously too, and since God is perfect Love he won't suddenly stab me in the back as though he were my personal enemy.


So there will be these repeat examinations.

What comforts me is that, while living on this earth, I've had any amount of time to observe the consequences of sin.

I can say with conviction, ''Sin doesn't interest me any more.''

It isn't interesting.

All it's done is give me a chance to develop my freedom.

But it isn't interesting.

In my sins certain factors have intervened which, I have to say, should properly be imputed to some angelic defender.

The principal of these intervening factors has been ignorance.

The majority of sins are committed out of ignorance.

The earth is the play-school of life and, without any risk of mistake, we can say that many of our sins are the stuff of ignorant, conceited children.

I remember an industrialist who was afraid of Hell; it was his only religion, and he came to seek me out, thinking to make a friend for himself in the calamitous days of *Dies irae dies illa*.

He was an industrialist but a big baby too.

He was the complete workaholic.

He added factory to factory as though this were the only thing worth doing.

He had no other ambition than to hear himself say, "Well done!"

A heart attack carried him off.

I'm sure the Lord gave him a little time to meditate on the relative value of things and on the priority of the family over work.

Possibly he had time to persuade himself that he could have lived more usefully if he'd taken a little more thought for his wife and spent more time developing common interests with his children.

Another factor to play a major role in sin is human weakness.

No, this biped without criteria is certainly no lion!

Human nature is fearfully weak.

Even the ancients used to say, "*Video meliora, proboque: deteriora sequor*" (I see what's good and approve it but do what's evil).

We can say there's no limit to human weakness; the sins of today bear irrefutable witness to this, especially where physical pleasures are concerned.

One might say our spiritual history walks the razor-edge of this sorry fact.

What a long time it takes for most people to attain equilibrium in their moral life!

Before celebrating the joy of victory over the senses!

That's how it is, and that's enough to humble us very thoroughly and teach us to pray for our salvation, without even mentioning the modern evils of drug abuse and sexual obsession.

There's no limit to the disaster; their families well know the havoc the drug-addict, the alchoholic and the sex maniac can wreak.

For many people the night of the senses doesn't take place on earth, and Jesus invites us not to pass judgement.

He himself came to save.

In the desert, the night of the senses is easier to endure since the body, which has been such a poor instrument to us, now rests in the earth and does penance to celebrate its final Mass.

Without ignorance, which is overcome by the light of God's approaching dawn; without weakness, which is overcome by humility in prayer, purgatory offers easier progress.

*"Remember not the former things, nor consider the things of old. Behold, I am doing a new thing.*

*"Now it springs forth; do you not perceive it?"*
(Is 43: 18–19).

So runs the prophetic text.

Yes, don't keep thinking about the negative things in your past; think about the new things.

What are they? They're what I ought to have done but didn't do on earth.

In purgatory we shall each compose our own lives as they would have been composed in the school of Jesus.

We shall want to do what we didn't do, we shall see what our true vocation was and is.

It won't be difficult to say, *"My God was right to say the human race was good."*

And it won't be difficult either to find time to prepare for sitting the exam once more.

# The mystery of Satan

or

My child, don't run away from me.
Be mine!
I'm appointing an excellent person to keep an eye on you: Satan.
He's the vilest of the vile, yet the most adept at making you understand things by means of the horror and ugliness of evil.

Since God, our God, the *One and Only*, the *Creator*, *Providence*, the *End*, the *Wonderful*, the *Victorious*, the *Merciful*, the *King*, the *Mighty One*, the *Great*, the *Just*, the *Splendid*, the *Invincible*, the *Holy One*, the *Resurrection*, the *Lord of Death*, the *Eternal*, the *First*, the *Last*, the *Almighty*, the *Truth*, the *Strong One*, the *Good*, the *Light*, the *Universal*, the *Perfect*, can tell us his children that *everything he has created is good*, it means that, *against the darkness of evil which we call Satan, he holds a winning card, mysterious but a winner.*

The fact of the matter is, Satan's a great mystery and we tax our brains over it in vain.

For my part however, I have by faith come to know two things about Satan of which I'm perfectly certain and to which I cling so as not to lose my balance.

*The first thing is that Satan exists.*

Jesus has told me so in the gospel and over what Jesus has told me I harbour no doubts.

Jesus calls him the Adversary, the Evil One, the Deceiver, the Accuser, Beelzebub, and that is enough for starters.

We know next to nothing about Satan.

Has he a face? Hasn't he got a face?

Has he horns and a tail as people in the Middle Ages thought? Being somewhat childish, they loved to make him ugly, really ugly, as ugly as they possibly could.

And they certainly succeeded!

But . . . I don't know.

What is certainly true is that he exists.

*The second thing I know for certain about him is that he isn't a "god" who can do whatever he likes.*

In the past, too much importance was attributed to the Devil, to all his works, to his power, if not to his "omnipotence".

All too many people were terrorised by his activities.

And the worst of it was that everything got mixed up: illness, sin, mystery, possession, visible and invisible riffraff, darkness, boundless terrors, incomprehension, ignorance, lack of faith, the will to acquire supernatural powers at any price, infantile superstitions, sophisticated untruths . . . you could go on indefinitely.

No, Satan isn't a god, not even the god of evil.

He's a servant, or rather a slave, of the One True God.

When he acts, he acts in accordance with God's will, which in any case governs what happens on earth for every creature.

Since God has stationed a watchdog as horrible as Satan at my door, I ought to realise that this watchdog has its mission to discharge and can be useful to me.

First of all, it prevents me from leaving the right path and compels me to stay at home, maybe in the very house of God.

If in the eyes of this raging dog I see the lamps of war with all its horror, I am urged towards peace.

If from the viscous and irrational body of this "*irrationality embodied*" arise temptations to sensuality and immodesty for me, I am straightaway urged to chastity.

The mystery of Satan is co-terminous with the whole mystery of evil and is quite impossible for us to understand.

Once we're in the kingdom, we shall see.

For now, it's sufficient that we should believe.

Yet, through the great gift of faith, we can in the here-and-now begin to experience something of his presence in us and in the world.

God makes use of him.

God makes use of evil, allows evil, because it's helpful to us in one way or another.

For example, Satan's presence alone, mere contact with diabolic reality, removes any wish for longer acquaintance with anything so horrible. And that's no small achievement.

No one who happens to catch a glimpse of Satan's leering face is likely to become his friend.

I don't believe there can be a single person in the world who could willingly, lovingly, endure his presence.

Then there's another very important thing we should grasp.

When we embark on the irrational road of sin and find ourselves bogged down in violence, lust, hatred and selfishness, to save us the Father doesn't turn to the angels and get them to come to the rescue.

The angels are too weak, too childlike, too smiling. They don't know much about evil and feel nervous about giving their whimpering subjects a hiding. That means us.

To reclaim the sinner, God sends Satan directly to administer the hiding.

Satan's a real professional who doesn't muck about; he knows his trade.

With the deadly means at his disposal, he lets Hell loose around us and blocks our path.

If we are gluttons, he wrecks our liver; if we are thieves, he lands us in gaol.

If we are sensualists, he brings us pain or worse; if we are self-centred, he suppresses our will to live lovingly; if we want war, he lets us have it cheap.

There's nothing Satan can't do to pander to our perverse tastes.

Indeed, it's hard to believe that it can actually be God prompting him to act against us but . . . it would seem to be so, so great is God's desire to save us.

That's how I see it.

And I think the Devil, the evil that terrifies us so, may be the most able of professionals at making us beware; the most illustrious of teachers to tell us from his own proven experience that God is God and beside him there is no other God.

He is certainly more effective than Mummy's winsome smiles at making us return home, permanently cured and with no further wish to escape.

With no Satan, one might run the risk of perishing, of wasting precious time.

With Satan at the door, no one wants to dally with mates like him with results so disastrous.

Who knows but one day we may be quite surprised to find ourselves thanking him for having done us a good turn with his terrors, his disasters and his ability to show us the way to heaven by pointing in the opposite direction: something by no means always negative.

To sum up, we can say that God seems to have

given us this "pain in the neck" to disgust us with evil and force us to stay at home, my home, my God's home.

If henceforth I no longer want to behave as the prodigal son behaved, I owe this also to Satan.

Yes, Satan helped me stay at home.


One word more about my brother Satan and about his lot of "helping" me by the unlikely path of evil and the terrors inspired by his mysterious activities on earth.

That Satan strikes terror by his very presence is a fact. You've only to attend an exorcism, where the Church fights to drive away the presence of the Devil — who's by no means nice and obedient — to feel the mystery send shudders running up and down your spine.

You need courage and a great deal of faith to keep up the fight.

But that's how it is, and there's no need to retreat. A Christian possesses the weapons of the Spirit, with which to blunt those of the Evil One.

A battle is rarely so illuminating as this: between the thirst for salvation consuming the human soul and the terror of defeat inspired by the presence and activity of Satan.

All ambiguities fall away and you realise that, over the totality of evil, God alone can be victorious. You experience the depths of human ineffectiveness and weakness, even to the point of feeling the very spasm of agony by which Satan is discomfited and put to flight.

This is one of the most tragic moments in the encounter between heaven and earth, between good and evil.

But even exorcism, which is the most dramatic

force the Church has at her disposal for putting the Evil One to flight, is weak and ineffectual when based solely on human reason and psychological factors. Only pure faith, tested as never before in the crucible of the infinite distance existing between the Spirit of God, the reality of God, the omnipotence of God, and everything else, evil included, can achieve total victory; otherwise, as Jesus says, Satan summons another seven spirits worse than himself and his victim's plight then becomes worse than before.

Such supernatural battles are only won when waged in that spirit of childlike faith that ought to be ours, as we recall Jesus's words to mind, "*Unless you become like children, you will never enter . . . never enter . . . never enter*" (Mt 18:3).

Spiritual childlikeness, passionate self-surrender to God our Father, is like a sharp arrow shooting invincibly between the mystery of God and the mystery of his opposite: evil.

This arrow has the power of overthrowing Satan and of releasing the song of truth in us: God is truly God.


Everyone knows that in this unusual period of the Church's history there is much talk about the Devil and his activities on earth and among the human race.

Matters have gone so far beyond the limits of the norm that many people are beginning to think they would like to study this mystery by prayer and collective meditation. There is talk of meetings, encounters, study-groups and opportunities for ecclesial experimentation.

I'm sure this is a fine idea and valuable for the

purposes of research into the truth and possible errors in this by no means simple subject.

In a pastoral spirit however I should like to underline some of the difficulties arising, due to fashion, curiosity and above all else widespread ignorance.

First of all, the times aren't easy and the lack of a genuine religious sense among the masses has given rise to a veritable mountain of superstitions, a tacky quest for the mysterious, a morbid curiosity inspiring research into myths and esoteric matters.

In this respect, our problems couldn't be greater. Wherever you go, sects are springing up, spiritualist meetings, fanatical and arrogant charlatans, the psychologically disordered, unbalanced Christians without the saving grace of faith, people athirst for spiritual novelties and vanities.

Add to all this a zeal to impress public opinion by means of the mass media and by the power of today's means of communication, by which public opinion is enslaved.

How are we to get ourselves out of such a dangerous, sticky mess?

It won't be easy; we shall need all the strength of faith and common sense if we are not to fail.

We shall need discernment and prudence if we are to distinguish between the charlatan who wants to impress the simple, and the man of God who still knows how to pray; between the deceiver who is only out to astound his audience, and the humble person seeking the truth about God.

In any case, I hope all those who may with prudence and discretion seek to understand something of this tremendous problem, will rid themselves beforehand of the vast accumulation of superstition, fanaticism and arrogance, and confront the problem of evil with childlike heart, and so be able to sing despite all difficulties the warcry of hope: God conquers.

# PART THREE

# PRAYING
# TO SEE OURSELVES
# IN A CLEARER LIGHT

A little guide for six days of prayer
with the Word of God

It seems right to end this book of conversations with God by inviting the reader to pray.

It's never a mistake to pray and I'm convinced that nothing can resist the power of prayer.

The prayers are arranged as short offices to be said either alone or in community, like morning and evening prayer.

The subject for the day will be found in the appropriate chapter of the book, as indicated.

The office begins with a psalm, followed by a reading from the Word of God.

# First day

## *Monday*

*God saw that it was good (Gen 1)*

## Morning

### Psalm 104: 1–35

1  Bless the Lord, O my soul!
    O Lord my God, thou art very great!
    Thou art clothed with honour and majesty,
2    who coverest thyself with light as with a
      garment,
    who hast stretched out the heavens like a tent,
3    who hast laid the beams of thy chambers on
      the waters,
    who makest the clouds thy chariot,
      who ridest on the wings of the wind,
4  who makest the winds thy messengers,
    fire and flame thy ministers.
5  Thou didst set the earth on its foundations,
    so that it should never be shaken.
6  Thou didst cover it with the deep as with a
    garment;
    the waters stood above the mountains.
7  At thy rebuke they fled;
    at the sound of thy thunder they took to
      flight.
8  The mountains rose, the valleys sank down
    to the place which thou didst appoint for
      them.
9  Thou didst set a bound which they should
    not pass,
    so that they might not again cover the earth.

10  Thou makest springs gush forth in the valleys;
        they flow between the hills,
11  they give drink to every beast of the field;
        the wild asses quench their thirst.
12  By them the birds of the air have their
            habitation;
        they sing among the branches.

13  From thy lofty abode thou waterest the
            mountains;
        the earth is satisfied with the fruit of thy work.
14  Thou dost cause the grass to grow for the
            cattle,
        and plants for man to cultivate,
    that he may bring forth food from the earth,
15      and wine to gladden the heart of man,
    oil to make his face shine,
        and bread to strengthen man's heart.

16  The trees of the Lord are watered abundantly,
        the cedars of Lebanon which he planted.
17  In them the birds build their nests;
        the stork has her home in the fir trees.
18  The high mountains are for the wild goats;
        the rocks are a refuge for the badgers.

19  Thou hast made the moon to mark the
            seasons;
        the sun knows its time for setting.
20  Thou makest darkness, and it is night,
        when all the beasts of the forest creep forth.
21  The young lions roar for their prey,
        seeking their food from God.
22  When the sun rises, they get them away
        and lie down in their dens.
23  Man goes forth to his work
        and to his labour until the evening.

24 O Lord, how manifold are thy works!
   In wisdom hast thou made them all;
25    the earth is full of thy creatures.
   Yonder is the sea, great and wide,
      which teems with things innumerable,
      living things both small and great.
26 There go the ships,
      and Leviathan which thou didst form to
         sport in it.

27 These all look to thee,
      to give them their food in due season.
28 When thou givest to them, they gather it up;
      when thou openest thy hand, they are filled
         with good things.
29 When thou hidest thy face, they are dismayed;
      when thou takest away their breath, they die
      and return to their dust.
30 When thou sendest forth thy Spirit, they are
         created;
      and thou renewest the face of the ground.

31 May the glory of the Lord endure for ever,
      may the Lord rejoice in his works,
32 who looks on the earth and it trembles,
      who touches the mountains and they smoke!
33 I will sing to the Lord as long as I live;
      I will sing praise to my God while I have
         being.
34 May my meditation be pleasing to him,
      for I rejoice in the Lord.

35 Let sinners be consumed from the earth,
      and let the wicked be no more!
   Bless the Lord, O my soul!
   Praise the Lord!

**Reading: Gen 1:1–31**

In the beginning God created the heavens and the earth. The earth was without form and void, and darkness was upon the face of the deep; and the Spirit of God was moving over the face of the waters.

And God said, "Let there be light"; and there was light. *And God saw that the light was good;* and God separated the light from the darkness. God called the light Day, and the darkness he called Night. And there was evening and there was morning, one day.

And God said, "Let there be a firmament in the midst of the waters, and let it separate the waters from the waters." And God made the firmament and separated the waters which were under the firmament from the waters which were above the firmament. And it was so. And God called the firmament Heaven. And there was evening and there was morning, a second day.

And God said, "Let the waters under the heavens be gathered together into one place, and let the dry land appear." And it was so. God called the dry land Earth, and the waters that were gathered together he called Seas. *And God saw that it was good.* And God said, "Let the earth put forth vegetation, plants yielding seed, and fruit trees bearing fruit in which is their seed, each according to its kind, upon the earth." And it was so. The earth brought forth vegetation, plants yielding seed according to their own kinds, and trees bearing fruit in which is their seed, each according to its kind. *And God saw that it was good.* And there was evening and there was morning, a third day.

And God said, "Let there be lights in the firmament of the heavens to separate the day from the night; and let them be for signs and for seasons and for days and years, and let them be lights in the firmament of the heavens to give light upon the earth." And it was so. And God made the two great lights, the greater light to rule the day, and the lesser light to rule the night; he made the stars also. And God set them in the firmament of the heavens to give light upon the earth, to rule over the day and over the night, and to separate the light from the darkness. *And God saw that it was good.* And there was evening and there was morning, a fourth day.

And God said, "Let the waters bring forth swarms of living creatures, and let birds fly above the earth across the firmament of the heavens." So God created the great sea monsters and every living creature that moves, with which the waters swarm, according to their kinds, and every winged bird according to its kind. *And God saw that it was good.* And God blessed them, saying, "Be fruitful and multiply and fill the waters in the seas, and let birds multiply on the earth." And there was evening and there was morning, a fifth day.

And God said, "Let the earth bring forth living creatures according to their kinds: cattle and creeping things and beasts of the earth according to their kinds." And it was so. And God made the beasts of the earth according to their kinds and the cattle according to their kinds, and everything that creeps upon the ground according to its kind. *And God saw that it was good.*

Then God said, "Let us make man in our image, after our likeness; and let them have dominion over the fish of the sea, and over the birds of the air, and over the cattle, and over all the earth, and over every creeping thing that creeps upon the earth."

So God created man in his own image,
in the image of God he created him;
male and female he created them.
And God blessed them, and God said to them,
"Be fruitful and multiply,
and fill the earth
and subdue it; and have dominion
over the fish of the sea
and over the birds of the air
and over every living thing
that moves upon the earth."
And God said, "Behold, I have given you every
plant yielding seed which is upon the face of all the
earth, and every tree with seed in its fruit; you shall
have them for food. And to every beast of the earth,
and to every bird of the air, and to everything that
creeps on the earth, everything that has the breath
of life, I have given every green plant for food." And
it was so. And God saw everything that he had
made, *and behold, it was very good.* And there was
evening and there was morning, a sixth day.

*Evening*

**Psalm 8:1–9**

1   O Lord, our Lord,
         how majestic is thy name in all the earth!

    Thou whose glory above the heavens is
            chanted
2        by the mouth of babes and infants,
    thou hast founded a bulwark because of thy
            foes,
         to still the enemy and the avenger.
3   When I look at thy heavens, the work of thy
            fingers,

the moon and the stars which thou hast
established;
4 what is man that thou art mindful of him,
and the son of man that thou dost care for
him?

5 Yet thou hast made him little less than God,
and dost crown him with glory and honour.
6 Thou hast given him dominion over the works
of thy hands;
thou hast put all things under his feet,
7 all sheep and oxen,
and also the beasts of the field,
8 the birds of the air, and the fish of the sea,
whatever passes along the paths of the sea.

9 O Lord, our Lord,
how majestic is thy name in all the earth!


**Reading: Rom 8:18–30**

I consider that the sufferings of this present time
are not worth comparing with the glory that is to
be revealed to us. For the creation waits with eager
longing for the revealing of the sons of God; for the
creation was subjected to futility, not of its own
will but by the will of him who subjected it in hope;
because the creation itself will be set free from its
bondage to decay and obtain the glorious liberty of
the children of God. We know that the whole creation has been groaning in travail together until now;
and not only the creation, but we ourselves, who
have the first fruits of the Spirit, groan inwardly as
we wait for adoption as sons, the redemption of our
bodies. For in this hope we were saved. Now hope
that is seen is not hope. For who hopes for what

121

he sees? But if we hope for what we do not see, we wait for it with patience.

Likewise the Spirit helps us in our weakness; for we do not know how to pray as we ought, but the Spirit himself intercedes for us with sighs too deep for words. And he who searches the hearts of men knows what is the mind of the Spirit, because the Spirit intercedes for the saints according to the will of God.

We know that in everything God works for good with those who love him, who are called according to his purpose. For those whom he foreknew he also predestined to be conformed to the image of his Son, in order that he might be the first-born among many brethren. And those whom he predestined he also called; and those whom he called he also justified; and those whom he justified he also glorified.

# Second day

## Tuesday

*I set before you good and evil: choose*

### Morning

### Psalm 37:1–26

1 Fret not yourself because of the wicked,
   be not envious of wrongdoers!
2 For they will soon fade like the grass,
   and wither like the green herb.
3 Trust in the Lord, and do good;
   so you will dwell in the land, and enjoy
   security.
4 Take delight in the Lord,
   and he will give you the desires of your
   heart.
5 Commit your way to the Lord;
   trust in him, and he will act.
6 He will bring forth your vindication as the
   light,
   and your right as the noonday.
7 Be still before the Lord, and wait patiently
   for him;
   fret not yourself over him who prospers in
   his way,
   over the man who carries out evil devices!
8 Refrain from anger, and forsake wrath!
   Fret not yourself; it tends only to evil.
9 For the wicked shall be cut off;
   but those who wait for the Lord shall possess
   the land.

10 Yet a little while, and the wicked will be no
      more;
    though you look well at his place, he will
      not be there.
11 But the meek shall possess the land,
    and delight themselves in abundant
      prosperity.

12 The wicked plots against the righteous,
    and gnashes his teeth at him;
13 but the Lord laughs at the wicked,
    for he sees that his day is coming.

14 The wicked draw the sword and bend their
      bows,
    to bring down the poor and needy,
    to slay those who walk uprightly;
15 their sword shall enter their own heart,
    and their bows shall be broken.

16 Better is a little that the righteous has
    than the abundance of many wicked.
17 For the arms of the wicked shall be broken;
    but the Lord upholds the righteous.

18 The Lord knows the days of the blameless,
    and their heritage will abide for ever;
19 they are not put to shame in evil times,
    in the days of famine they have abundance.
20 But the wicked perish;
    the enemies of the Lord are like the glory
      of the pastures,
    they vanish — like smoke they vanish away.

21 The wicked borrows, and cannot pay back,
    but the righteous is generous and gives;
22 for those blessed by the Lord shall possess
      the land,
    but those cursed by him shall be cut off.

23 The steps of a man are from the Lord,
    and he establishes him in whose way he
      delights;
24 though he fall, he shall not be cast headlong,
    for the Lord is the stay of his hand.
25 I have been young, and now am old;
    yet I have not seen the righteous forsaken
    or his children begging bread.
26 He is ever giving liberally and lending,
    and his children become a blessing.

**Reading: Deut 30:15–20**

"See, I have set before you this day life and good, death and evil. If you obey the commandments of the Lord your God which I command you this day, by loving the Lord your God, by walking in his ways, and by keeping his commandments and his statutes and his ordinances, then you shall live and multiply, and the Lord your God will bless you in the land which you are entering to take possession of it. But if your heart turns away, and you will not hear, but are drawn away to worship other gods and serve them, I declare to you this day, that you shall perish; you shall not live long in the land which you are going over the Jordan to enter and possess. I call heaven and earth to witness against you this day, that I have set before you life and death, blessing and curse; therefore choose life, that you and your descendants may live, loving the Lord your God, obeying his voice, and cleaving to him; for that means life to you and length of days, that you may dwell in the land which the Lord swore to your fathers, to Abraham, to Isaac, and to Jacob, to give them."

*Evening*

## Psalm 128:1–6

1  Blessed is every one who fears the Lord,
   who walks in his ways!
2  You shall eat the fruit of the labour of your
      hands;
   you shall be happy, and it shall be well
      with you.

3  Your wife will be like a fruitful vine
      within your house;
   your children will be like olive shoots
      around your table.
4  Lo, thus shall the man be blessed
      who fears the Lord.

5  The Lord bless you from Zion!
   May you see the prosperity of Jerusalem
      all the days of your life!
6  May you see your children's children!
      Peace be upon Israel!

## Reading: Gal 5:1–18

For freedom Christ has set us free; stand fast
therefore, and do not submit again to a yoke of
slavery.

Now I, Paul, say to you that if you receive circumcision, Christ will be of no advantage to you.
I testify again to every man who receives circumcision that he is bound to keep the whole law. You
are severed from Christ, you who would be justified
by the law; you have fallen away from grace. For
through the Spirit, by faith, we wait for the hope
of righteousness. For in Christ Jesus neither

126

circumcision nor uncircumcision is of any avail, but faith working through love. You were running well; who hindered you from obeying the truth? This persuasion is not from him who called you. A little leaven leavens the whole lump. I have confidence in the Lord that you will take no other view than mine; and he who is troubling you will bear his judgment, whoever he is. But if I, brethren, still preach circumcision, why am I still persecuted? In that case the stumbling block of the cross has been removed. I wish those who unsettle you would mutilate themselves!

For you were called to freedom, brethren; only do not use your freedom as an opportunity for the flesh, but through love be servants of one another. For the whole law is fulfilled in one word, *"You shall love your neighbour as yourself."* But if you bite and devour one another take heed that you are not consumed by one another.

But I say, walk by the Spirit, and do not gratify the desires of the flesh. For the desires of the flesh are against the Spirit, and the desires of the Spirit are against the flesh; for these are opposed to each other, to prevent you from doing what you would. But if you are led by the Spirit you are not under the law.

# Third day

## *Wednesday*

*Human beings, my children*

*Morning*

### Psalm 118:1–9

1   O give thanks to the Lord, for he is good;
     his steadfast love endures for ever!
2   Let Israel say,
     "His steadfast love endures for ever."
3   Let the house of Aaron say,
     "His steadfast love endures for ever."
4   Let those who fear the Lord say,
     "His steadfast love endures for ever."
5   Out of my distress I called on the Lord;
     the Lord answered me and set me free.
6   With the Lord on my side I do not fear.
     What can man do to me?
7   The Lord is on my side to help me;
     I shall look in triumph on those who hate me.
8   It is better to take refuge in the Lord
     than to put confidence in man.
9   It is better to take refuge in the Lord
     than to put confidence in princes.

### Reading: Rom 8:14–17

For all who are led by the Spirit of God are sons of God. For you did not receive the spirit of slavery to fall back into fear, but you have received the spirit of sonship. When we cry, "Abba! Father!" it is the Spirit himself bearing witness with our spirit that we are children of God, and if children, then heirs, heirs of God and fellow heirs with Christ, provided we suffer with him in order that we may also be glorified with him.

*Evening*

## Psalm 131:1–3

1  O Lord, my heart is not lifted up,
     my eyes are not raised too high;
   I do not occupy myself with things
     too great and too marvellous for me.
2  But I have calmed and quieted my soul,
     like a child quieted at its mother's breast;
     like a child that is quieted is my soul.
3  O Israel, hope in the Lord
     from this time forth and for evermore.

## Reading: Gal 4:1–7

I mean that the heir, as long as he is a child, is no better than a slave, though he is the owner of all the estate; but he is under guardians and trustees until the date set by the father. So with us; when we were children, we were slaves to the elemental spirits of the universe. But when the time had fully come, God sent forth his Son, born of woman, born under the law, to redeem those who were under the law, so that we might receive adoption as sons. And because you are sons, God has sent the Spirit of his Son into our hearts, crying, "Abba! Father!" So through God you are no longer a slave but a son, and if a son then an heir.

# Fourth day

## *Thursday*

*Morning*

### Psalm 2:1–12

1   Why do the nations conspire,
    and the peoples plot in vain?
2   The kings of the earth set themselves,
    and the rulers take counsel together,
    against the Lord and his anointed, saying,
3   "Let us burst their bonds asunder,
    and cast their cords from us."

4   He who sits in the heavens laughs;
    the Lord has them in derision.
5   Then he will speak to them in his wrath,
    and terrify them in his fury, saying,
6   "I have set my king
    on Zion, my holy hill."

7   I will tell of the decree of the Lord:
    He said to me, "You are my son,
    today I have begotten you.
8   Ask of me, and I will make the nations your
    heritage,
    and the ends of the earth your possession.
9   You shall break them with a rod of iron,
    and dash them in pieces like a potter's
    vessel."

10   Now therefore, O kings, be wise;
    be warned, O rulers of the earth.

<sup>11</sup> Serve the Lord with fear,
    with trembling kiss his feet,
<sup>12</sup> lest he be angry, and you perish in the way;
    for his wrath is quickly kindled.

Blessed are all who take refuge in him.

## Reading: Jn 1:1–18

In the beginning was the Word, and the Word was with God, and the Word was God. He was in the beginning with God; all things were made through him, and without him was not anything made that was made. In him was life, and the life was the light of men. The light shines in the darkness, and the darkness has not overcome it.

There was a man sent from God, whose name was John. He came for testimony, to bear witness to the light, that all might believe through him. He was not the light, but came to bear witness to the light.

The true light that enlightens every man was coming into the world. He was in the world, and the world was made through him, yet the world knew him not. He came to his own home, and his own people received him not. But to all who received him, who believed in his name, he gave power to become children of God; who were born, not of blood nor of the will of the flesh nor of the will of man, but of God.

And the Word became flesh and dwelt among us, full of grace and truth; we have beheld his glory, glory as of the only Son from the Father. (John bore witness to him, and cried, ''This was he of whom I said, 'He who comes after me ranks before me, for he was before me.' '') And from his fullness

131

have we all received, grace upon grace. For the law was given through Moses; grace and truth came through Jesus Christ. No one has ever seen God; the only Son, who is in the bosom of the Father, he has made him known.

*Evening*

## Psalm 110:1–7

*A Psalm of David*

1 The Lord says to my lord:
    "Sit at my right hand,
    till I make your enemies your footstool."

2 The Lord sends forth from Zion
    your mighty sceptre.
    Rule in the midst of your foes!
3 Your people will offer themselves freely
    on the day you lead your host
    upon the holy mountains.

From the womb of the morning
    like dew your youth will come to you.
4 The Lord has sworn
    and will not change his mind,
    "You are a priest for ever
    after the order of Melchizedek."

5 The Lord is at your right hand;
    he will shatter kings on the day of his
        wrath.
6 He will execute judgement among the nations,
    filling them with corpses;
    he will shatter chiefs
    over the wide earth.
7 He will drink from the brook by the way;
    therefore he will lift up his head.

**Reading: Mt 17:1–8**

And after six days Jesus took with him Peter and James and John his brother, and led them up a high mountain apart. And he was transfigured before them, and his face shone like the sun, and his garments became white as light. And behold, there appeared to them Moses and Elijah, talking with him. And Peter said to Jesus, "Lord, it is well that we are here; if you wish, I will make three booths here, one for you and one for Moses and one for Elijah." He was still speaking, when lo, a bright cloud overshadowed them, and a voice from the cloud said, "This is my beloved Son, with whom I am well pleased; listen to him." When the disciples heard this, they fell on their faces, and were filled with awe. But Jesus came and touched them, saying, "Rise, and have no fear." And when they lifted up their eyes, they saw no one but Jesus only.

# Fifth day

## *Friday*

*Do not be overcome by evil, but*
*overcome evil with good*

## *Morning*

### Psalm 36:1–12

1 Transgression speaks to the wicked
    deep in his heart;
there is no fear of God
    before his eyes.
2 For he flatters himself in his own eyes
    that his iniquity cannot be found out and
      hated.
3 The words of his mouth are mischief and
      deceit;
    he has ceased to act wisely and do good.
4 He plots mischief while on his bed;
    he sets himself in a way that is not good;
    he spurns not evil.

5 Thy steadfast love, O Lord, extends to the
      heavens,
    thy faithfulness to the clouds.
6 Thy righteousness is like the mountains of
      God,
    thy judgments are like the great deep;
    man and beast thou savest, O Lord.

7 How precious is thy steadfast love, O God!
    The children of men take refuge in the
      shadow of thy wings.
8 They feast on the abundance of thy house,
    and thou givest them drink from the river
      of thy delights.

9  For with thee is the fountain of life;
       in thy light do we see light.
10  O continue thy steadfast love to those who
           know thee,
       and thy salvation to the upright of heart!
11  Let not the foot of arrogance come upon me,
       nor the hand of the wicked drive me away.
12  There the evildoers lie prostrate,
       they are thrust down, unable to rise.

### Reading: Lk 4:1–13

And Jesus, full of the Holy Spirit, returned from the Jordan, and was led by the Spirit for forty days in the wilderness, tempted by the devil. And he ate nothing in those days; and when they were ended, he was hungry. The devil said to him, "If you are the Son of God, command this stone to become bread." And Jesus answered him, "It is written, *'Man shall not live by bread alone.'* " And the devil took him up, and showed him all the kingdoms of the world in a moment of time, and said to him, "To you I will give all this authority and their glory; for it has been delivered to me, and I give it to whom I will. If you, then, will worship me, it shall all be yours." And Jesus answered him, "It is written,
   *'You shall worship the Lord your God,*
   *and him* only *shall you serve.'* "
And he took him to Jerusalem, and set him on the pinnacle of the temple, and said to him, "If you are the Son of God, throw yourself down from here; for it is written,
   *'He will give his angels charge of you, to*
       *guard you,'*

and
*'On their hands they will bear you up,
lest you strike your foot against a stone.'* "
And Jesus answered him, "It is said, *'You shall not
tempt the Lord your God.'* " And when the devil
had ended every temptation, he departed from him
until an opportune time.

*Evening*

## Psalm 52:1–9

1   Why do you boast, O mighty man,
        of mischief done against the godly?
2       All the day you are plotting destruction.
    Your tongue is like a sharp razor,
        you worker of treachery.
3   You love evil more than good,
        and lying more than speaking the truth.

4   You love all words that devour,
        O deceitful tongue.

5   But God will break you down for ever;
        he will snatch and tear you from your tent;
        he will uproot you from the land of the
            living.
6   The righteous shall see, and fear,
        and shall laugh at him, saying,
7   "See the man who would not make God his
            refuge,
        but trusted in the abundance of his riches,
        and sought refuge in his wealth!"

8   But I am like a green olive tree
        in the house of God.
    I trust in the steadfast love of God
        for ever and ever.

9   I will thank thee for ever,
      because thou hast done it.
   I will proclaim thy name, for it is good,
      in the presence of the godly.

### Reading: Rom 12:9–21

Let love be genuine; hate what is evil, hold fast to what is good; love one another with brotherly affection; outdo one another in showing honour. Never flag in zeal, be aglow with the Spirit, serve the Lord. Rejoice in your hope, be patient in tribulation, be constant in prayer. Contribute to the needs of the saints, practise hospitality.

Bless those who persecute you; bless and do not curse them. Rejoice with those who rejoice, weep with those who weep. Live in harmony with one another; do not be haughty, but associate with the lowly; never be conceited. Repay no one evil for evil, but *take thought for what is noble in the sight of all*. If possible, so far as it depends upon you, live peaceably with all. Beloved, never avenge yourselves, but leave it to the wrath of God; for it is written' *"Vengeance is mine, I will repay, says the Lord."* No, *"if your enemy is hungry, feed him; if he is thirsty, give him drink; for by so doing you will heap burning coals upon his head."* Do not be overcome by evil, but overcome evil with good.

# Sixth day

## Saturday

*Thou in me and I in thee so that we may
be perfectly united*

### Morning

#### Psalm 62:1–12

1 For God alone my soul waits in silence;
    from him comes my salvation.
2 He only is my rock and my salvation,
    my fortress; I shall not be greatly moved.

3 How long will you set upon a man
    to shatter him, all of you,
    like a leaning wall, a tottering fence?
4 They only plan to thrust him down from his
    eminence.
    They take pleasure in falsehood.
They bless with their mouths,
    but inwardly they curse.

5 For God alone my soul waits in silence,
    for my hope is from him.
6 He only is my rock and my salvation,
    my fortress; I shall not be shaken.
7 On God rests my deliverance and my honour;
    my mighty rock, my refuge is God.

8 Trust in him at all times, O people;
    pour out your heart before him;
    God is a refuge for us.
9 Men of low estate are but a breath,
    men of high estate are a delusion;

in the balances they go up;
    they are together lighter than a breath.
10  Put no confidence in extortion,
    set no vain hopes on robbery;
    if riches increase, set not your heart on
      them.
11  Once God has spoken;
    twice have I heard this;
    that power belongs to God;
12    and that to thee, O Lord, belongs steadfast
      love.
    For thou dost requite a man
    according to his work.

## Reading: Jn 15:1–17

"I am the true vine, and my Father is the vinedresser. Every branch of mine that bears no fruit, he takes away, and every branch that does bear fruit he prunes, that it may bear more fruit. You are already made clean by the word which I have spoken to you. Abide in me, and I in you. As the branch cannot bear fruit by itself, unless it abides in the vine, neither can you, unless you abide in me. I am the vine, you are the branches. He who abides in me, and I in him, he it is that bears much fruit, for apart from me you can do nothing. If a man does not abide in me, he is cast forth as a branch and withers; and the branches are gathered, thrown into the fire and burned. If you abide in me, and my words abide in you, ask whatever you will, and it shall be done for you. By this my Father is glorified, that you bear much fruit, and so prove to be my disciples. As the Father has loved me, so have I loved you; abide in my love. If you keep my commandments, you will abide in my love, just as I have kept my Father's commandments and abide in his love. These things I have spoken to you, that my joy may be in you, and that your joy may be full.

"This is my commandment, that you love one another as I have loved you. Greater love has no man than this, that a man lay down his life for his friends. You are my friends if you do what I command you. No longer do I call you servants, for the servant does not know what his master is doing; but I have called you friends, for all that I have heard from my Father I have made known to you. You did not choose me, but I chose you and appointed you that you should go and bear fruit and that your fruit should abide; so that whatever you ask the Father in my name, he may give it to you. This I command you, to love one another.

*Evening*

## Psalm 125:1–5

1 Those who trust in the Lord are like Mount Zion,
   which cannot be moved, but abides for ever.
2 As the mountains are round about Jerusalem,
   so the Lord is round about his people,
   from this time forth and for evermore.
3 For the sceptre of wickedness shall not rest
   upon the land allotted to the righteous,
   lest the righteous put forth
   their hands to do wrong.
4 Do good, O Lord, to those who are good,
   and to those who are upright in their hearts!
5 But those who turn aside upon their crooked ways
   the Lord will lead away with evildoers!
   Peace be in Israel!

### Reading: Jn 17:1–26

When Jesus had spoken these words, he lifted up his eyes to heaven and said, "Father, the hour has come; glorify thy Son that the Son may glorify thee, since thou hast given him power over all flesh, to give eternal life to all whom thou hast given him. And this is eternal life, that they know thee the only true God, and Jesus Christ whom thou hast sent. I glorified thee on earth, having accomplished the work which thou gavest me to do; and now, Father, glorify thou me in thy own presence with the glory which I had with thee before the world was made.

"I have manifested thy name to the men whom thou gavest me out of the world; thine they were, and thou gavest them to me, and they have kept thy word. Now they know that everything that thou hast given me is from thee; for I have given them the words which thou gavest me, and they have received them and know in truth that I came from thee; and they have believed that thou didst send me. I am praying for them; I am not praying for the world but for those whom thou hast given me, for they are thine; all mine are thine, and thine are mine, and I am glorified in them. And now I am no more in the world, but they are in the world, and I am coming to thee. Holy Father, keep them in thy name, which thou hast given me, that they may be one, even as we are one.

While I was with them, I kept them in thy name, which thou hast given me; I have guarded them, and none of them is lost but the son of perdition, that the scripture might be fulfilled. But now I am coming to thee; and these things I speak in the world, that they may have my joy fulfilled in themselves. I have given them thy word; and the world has hated them because they are not of the world, even as I am not of the world.

I do not pray that thou shouldst take them out of the world, but that thou shouldst keep them from the evil one. They are not of the world, even as I am not of the world. Sanctify them in the truth; thy word is truth. As thou didst send me into the world, so I have sent them into the world. And for their sake I consecrate myself, that they also may be consecrated in truth.

"I do not pray for these only, but also for those who believe in me through their word, that they may all be one; even as thou, Father, art in me, and I in thee, that they also may be in us, so that the world may believe that thou hast sent me.

The glory which thou hast given me I have given to them, that they may be one even as we are one, I in them and thou in me, that they may become perfectly one, so that the world may know that thou hast sent me and hast loved them even as thou hast loved me.

Father, I desire that they also, whom thou hast given me, may be with me where I am, to behold my glory which thou hast given me in thy love for me before the foundation of the world.

O righteous Father, the world has not known thee, but I have known thee; and these know that thou hast sent me. I made known to them thy name, and I will make it known, that the love with which thou hast loved me may be in them, and I in them.''